Thomas Cook
INTERNATIONAL
top 50
SKI RESORTS

Thomas Cook
INTERNATIONAL
top 50
Ski RESORTS

ARNOLD WILSON
THE FINANCIAL TIMES
SKI CORRESPONDENT
Foreword by Peter Lunn

Webb & Bower

FOR JULIA

*'When I am an old man, I will look back on
Christmas 1923 as the day when, to all intents
and purposes, I was born. I don't think anyone
has* lived *until they have been on ski.'*

ANDREW IRVINE
Disappeared on Everest, 1924.

First published in Great Britain 1989 by
Webb & Bower (Publishers) Limited
5 Cathedral Close, Exeter, Devon EX1 1EZ
in association with The Thomas Cook Group Limited,
Thorpe Wood, Peterborough PE3 6SB

First impression 1989
Second impression 1990

Published in association with the Penguin Group
Penguin Books Ltd, Registered Offices: Harmondsworth,
Middlesex, England
Viking Penguin Inc, 375 Hudson Street,
New York 10014, US
Penguin Books Australia Ltd, Ringwood, Victoria, Australia
Penguin Books Canada Ltd, 2801 John Street, Markham,
Ontario, Canada L3R 1B4
Penguin Books (NZ) Ltd, 182–190 Wairau Road,
Auckland 10, New Zealand

Designed by Sue Stainton
Production by Nick Facer/Rob Kendrew

British Library Cataloguing in Publication Data
Wilson, Arnold, *1931 –*
    Thomas Cook international top fifty ski resorts
    1. Skiing resorts, – Visitors' guides
    I. Title
    910',2'02

ISBN 0–86350–377–2

Typeset in Great Britain by J&L Composition Ltd, Filey,
North Yorkshire

Colour reproduction by Peninsular Repro Service Ltd,
Exeter, Devon

Printed and bound in Italy by LEGO

Contents

Foreword

I am delighted to contribute a few well-chosen words to this book, particularly as my grandfather, Henry Lunn, played an important part in popularizing the sport of skiing. He was the great pioneer of recreational winter sports – he took the first winter sports party, some fifty people, to Chamonix in December 1898. He later transferred his interests to Switzerland, where he succeeded in persuading fifteen summer resorts that he could bring them sufficient business to justify remaining open during the winter months. Among the resorts to be in the vanguard of what was to become the winter-sports revolution were Klosters, Wengen and Mürren. In writing this Foreword, I am paying indirect tribute to my grandfather, a man who amazingly never skied, but to whom so many people owe skiing happiness.

As hardly anybody knew in 1898, but as people all over the world know now, downhill skiing *does* bring very great happiness. I find it fitting that this book should begin with the quotation from Andrew Irvine about his love for skiing – a brief comment written sixty-five years ago but so expressive that it is forever etched on the memory. Andrew Irvine was no stranger to adventure. Before his short life so tragically ended, he had explored Spitsbergen, rowed in the winning Oxford boat and had been selected for the Everest expedition. It was, however, skiing that he singled out as the supreme experience. I recall my friendship with Andrew Irvine with great affection. He and I were both competitors in an early Mürren slalom. As was then customary, the second run was on a different course and on soft snow. I remember then how I enjoyed the powder-snow skiing, as I still do today. I also knew as I went down the course that I was racing well. I went through what I thought to be the finishing gate and turned towards my parents expecting their congratulations. I then saw my mother standing beside the finishing gate, pointing mutely at it. After scrambling through I burst into tears. Of course, my parents reprimanded me severely for treating sporting misfortune as an excuse for uncontrolled lament. I finished third in the race and there hangs in my home a photograph of myself, nine years old and still looking somewhat grumpy, standing beside the winner, Andrew Irvine. Shortly after the race Andrew Irvine left for Everest; he had the very great kindness to write two long letters to me from there, one of which outlined the plan for the attempt on the summit which was to cost him his life.

Andrew Irvine was young and very fit. If I can make any contribution to the sport it is perhaps to prove from personal experience that a passion for skiing survives old age and decrepitude. I was over seventy when both my legs were broken in a car crash; the next morning the surgeon told my daughter that I would never ski again. I *do* still ski, but very badly, and to manage even that I have to ski on much shorter skies.

Despite the physical limitations, I still enjoy skiing so much that during one recent winter I was able to ski every day for four months, and yet felt keen regret when I took off my skis for the last time. Skiing is a healthy addiction and, once hooked, there is no cure. It has certainly played a major part in my life, and I have none other than my grandfather to blame for inspiring me, and millions of others since, to take up the habit.

PETER LUNN

Introduction

Fifteen years ago, when I was thirty, a friend who edited a ski magazine asked me if I would like to visit the Swiss resort of Haute Nendaz and write an article about it. I dutifully packed my wife and two eldest daughters, Melissa and Samantha, into the car and set out.

Having skied once before – on a school outing to Andermatt when I was sixteen – I was confident that I would quickly master not only the slopes of Nendaz, but also those of neighbouring Verbier.

On the first day I suffered bruised and possibly cracked ribs but this did not deter me from attempting a difficult run under the cable car at the end of the day. To my humiliation, my skiing was so bad that an alarmed piste patrol man watching my wild attempts to turn, decided to rescue me. I was determined to learn properly.

Over the intervening years, I have enjoyed some wonderful adventures in the mountains of every continent, sharing the delights of more than two hundred resorts with a handful of colleagues who have become close friends. I have also had the enormous privilege of skiing – sometimes alone, sometimes accompanied by two or three friends – with some of the world's greatest guides and instructors.

Men like Daniel Hansjacob who scared, enthralled, and cajoled our party by taking us down our first couloir in Val d'Isère. Jean-Marc Boivin, who has skied impossible descents like the Matterhorn and Les Drus (Chamonix) and recently parapented from Everest. It was Jean-Marc who introduced me to helicopter skiing and whose colleague Jean-Paul Ollagnier, with noble assistance from the brawny Eddie Laxton, rescued me from a crevasse on the Italian side of Mont Blanc.

Men like Joe Mellaun from St Anton, who won the World Powder 8 Championships in 1988, and taught us the most meticulous snowcraft during some quite astonishing days of powder skiing – some from a helicopter – and introduced us to one of the most challenging runs in the Alps: the steep descent off the Valluga's north face down to Zürs.

Giles Claret-Tournier of Chamonix, who cut footholds in the seracs with his ice axe and lowered us by rope down ice walls as he took three of the group down the Vallée Blanche – normally a 'tourist' run – by such an exotic route on such an exceptionally beautiful day and in such enthralling conditions that we shall remember it for the rest of our lives. There is no experience on earth that I know of that compares with being high in the mountains with a few close friends, being shepherded down huge, sunny and silent snowfields by a caring and skilful mountain guide.

My choice of resorts in this book reflects this. I have tried to be as up-to-date as possible with details of runs and lifts, but like glaciers, ski resorts are constantly on the move and every year new runs are opened and new lifts are added. The 'Ski Facts' panels usually deal with a resort's *local* skiing, but in the text I have sometimes referred to an entire region of available skiing. The Americans like their mountains in feet rather than metres and I have kept it that way. The selection of resorts is very much a personal one and you may well have your own ideas about what should have been included in the book. I have chosen resorts that excite me either because of their dramatic scenery or their exhilarating skiing - preferably both.

These resorts are the places that inspire. And, on those magical days when the sky is cloudless, the space is infinite, the mountains stand out in jagged, gigantic magnificence, the snow is perfect and the sun warms the chilled mountain air, merely being there can be a quite mystical experience.

ARNOLD WILSON

GASTEIN VALLEY

The Gastein Valley, high in the Hohe Tauern mountains in Salzburgerland, is full of places called something-Gastein which can be quite confusing even when you try to ski there, let alone when you have never been near the place(s). Starting at the lowest of them, Dorfgastein, you work your way up through Bad Hofgastein and Badgastein onwards and upwards to Sportgastein. By consensus the resort takes its name from the town of Bad Hofgastein (the oldest) which is probably as good a Gastein as any.

It is actually very good. Rather like Ischgl (see page 12) Bad Hofgastein (originally called Ze Hove, but there are no obvious links with Sussex) and Badgastein are something of an Austrian secret – immensely popular with the Austrians themselves, but not well known to British skiers.

'Research', says the Salzburgerland tourist office with teutonic curtness, 'has established that vacationing in the mountains is good for you.' Apart from its beautiful mountains, lots of natural hot water, and the famous rushing waters of the River Ache cascading through the steep valley which Badgastein and its steeply tiered buildings occupy, the region has something else, rather sinister-sounding, going for it: radon gas.

Although it was important in the Middle Ages as a gold and silver mining area, the resort was made famous – as its 'Bad' prefix implies – by its thermal waters which to this day provides hot water for some of the town's hotels.

They also heat a wonderful public swimming bath (the largest in Austria) where you can swim outside into the cold night air and still keep warm in temperatures around seventy-five degrees as you survey a star-spangled sky, the occasional pencil beam of an airliner's lights or even find yourself steaming in a flurry of freshly falling snow.

According to the official version, the hot springs originated with water that 'fell to earth 3,500 years ago' and was enriched by trace elements and radon

Soak in the magnificent scenery in a deck-chair of your own invention!

gas in the 'mineral-rich rock formations' of the Graukogel. Local legend has it that the Gasteiner springs were discovered in the seventh century when two hunters chasing a wounded stag found it intuitively nursing its injuries in a steaming pool.

Having been reading about radon gas killing residents in America and even Cornwall, I rang a Doctor Schuster in Gastein for some clarification. He assured me that in small doses – rather like aspirin – radon was good for you, even though it could be fatal after lengthy exposure. Not being a medical expert I have to take his word for it. Certainly thousands of Austrians and Germans do.

The waters are said to promote cell growth and help disorders such as rheumatism, arthritis, sciatica, irregular circulation, diabetes, gout, bad gums, tuberculosis, asthma, sinus and respiratory disorders, premature ageing and even impotence.

The facilities in Badgastein include a 'therapeutic-gallery' hewn out of the rocks in which guests stretch out in a natural sauna, with doctors, masseuses and physiotherapists in attendance. The 'cure' is endorsed by the Research Institute of the Austrian Academy of Science, and is taken so seriously that it is possible to receive such treatment through certain German health insurance policies.

Over the centuries, we are told, those eager to try the treatment have included kings, emperors, princes, heads of state, composers, church leaders, and, more recently, 'international celebrities.'

Personally I find skiing an equally rewarding panacea: the skiing here is very wide open, picturesque and sunny, and there is a great deal of it (around 250 kilometres (155 miles) of groomed runs, served by more than sixty lifts plus acres of good off-piste, some of it side-by-side with the pisted runs). The only real snag is that it does not all link up terribly well, and to explore the full circuit you will need the help of the local bus service.

The Gastein Valley: picturesque and sunny skiing – and lots of it.

The most demanding skiing is at Sportgastein (a very useful if sometimes cold and windy high-altitude ski area when conditions lower down are not so good) and off the Stubnerkogel and Graukogel at Badgastein. The Schlossalm, a large bowl above the tree-line, provides most of Bad Hofgastein's skiing.

From the Stubnerkogel there is an exhilarating north-face off-piste run down to Heilstollen, but you will need to catch a bus back from Bockstein. Also from the Stubnerkogel, there is a classic red run, eleven kilometres long, descending to Angertal. Another good run for intermediates is the long run behind the Schlossalm down to Kitzstein. The Gastein Valley is only about ninety minutes' drive from Salzburg.

As for the cure for impotence, I would put my money on a good day's skiing rather than any fancy gas.

Bad Gastein offers a cure for everything, plus cheap hot water.

SKI FACTS

RESORT HEIGHT	1850 m
RANGE	1850 – 2500 m
BLACK RUNS	6
RED RUNS	39
BLUE RUNS	14
TOTAL	59
PISTES	250 km
LIFTS	50
LONGEST RUN	11 km

ISCHGL

*I*schgl Geniet Volop Van De Sneeuw! That is Dutch for Ischgl Wallows In The Snow. It has a wonderful ring to it – and the tourist office, who wish to broadcast this wallowing in as many languages as possible, are quite right to be proud of their resort, which they also market as 'Winter Has A Star.'

If it were not for the majestic resort of St Anton, Ischgl, in the Paznuan Valley would be my favourite Austrian resort. The slopes are vast and wide open, the runs – either in high, open bowls or through lower wooded slopes – are sweeping and sunny, and the whole arena is a sheer joy to ski.

Ischgl – originally 'Yscla' – is the jewel in the Silvretta Range which separates Austria from Switzerland. And indeed some of the best skiing in the resort is actually over the border. You can even ski via Palinkopf to the Swiss duty-free area of Samnaun with a back-pack (they sell them there if you forget to take one) and pick up some duty-free gifts.

A little like Wengen, the skiing is wonderfully picturesque without being terribly testing. The runs from Pardatschgrat back down to Ischgl are among the more demanding, but even they are only red. There is also some excellent skiing off the Greitspitz and the Palinkopf.

The lifts to Holltal take you to what are probably the most testing and enjoyable runs – black and beautiful, with some good off-piste thrown in. There is a pleasant excursion through the trees to Bodenalp. None of these is what I would call really challenging. But experts can and do enjoy skiing in Ischgl for all that.

Somehow it is such great recreational skiing, with such delightful scenery that it does not seem to matter that there are few really difficult runs. And there is some excellent off-piste skiing.

Ischgl offers a magnificent variety of skiing for all the family.

The only complaints I had involved the temperature and the queues. The skiing on the Austrian side – which faces north-west – was so cold that the immediate task of the day was to get over the hills and far away into Switzerland where the slopes face south and east as quickly as possible, and ski in comparitive warmth.

And queuing was not only a problem in the morning, getting up the mountain. It was also irritating in the evening trying to get skis and person on to the skibus travelling to my hotel in neighbouring Galtur. Often one would successfully battle to get one's skis into the rack at the back of the bus only to find the driver trying to drive off before you had actually got *yourself* on.

However, new lifts have eased the queuing problems and anyway once you are up and skiing these considerations soon disappear into the ether until the last run of the day, by which time you have probably had such a wonderful day's skiing that you do not really care about the tribulations awaiting you down the mountain.

For some reason Ischgl is not terribly familiar to the British although the Scandinavians and the Germans know all about it. Many of the Germans sweep in from other areas such as Galtur, a pleasant, much more rustic and much smaller satellite (one of the places visited on skis by Hemingway), just down the road. It is not linked but there is a ski bus and the lift pass covers both, as well as Kappl and See.

In some ways (it is cosier and prettier) Galtur is a charming alternative location for accommodation, although I remember the church bells clanging out across the cold and frosty snowfields well before dawn. Perhaps this gave Hemingway the idea for the title of his novel *For Whom The Bell Tolls*.

Ischgl is situated at 1400 metres (4,600 feet) and the skiing goes as high as 2800 metres (9,186 feet). There are some thirty-five lifts serving 150 kilometres (93 miles) of skiing. There is a choice of three gondolas to take you up to the main skiing area. Two of them converge at Idalp, a meeting point from which you can ski back to Ischgl or descend into the Swiss skiing area.

Ischgl: one of the Austrian's own favourites. Hemingway passed this way too.

SKI FACTS

RESORT HEIGHT	1400 m
RANGE	1400 – 2864 m
BLACK RUNS	5
RED RUNS	32
BLUE RUNS	20
TOTAL	57
PISTES	150 km
LIFTS	34
LONGEST RUN	9 km

KITZBUHEL

Height it may not have. But like Dudley Moore, Kitzbühel has just about everything else going for it. Even a towering inferno – as Mr Moore likes to describe his former wives – in the shape of the dreaded Streif descent of the Hahnenkamm.

If ever a ski resort made up for its one natural defect – a lack of altitude (which it can scarcely be blamed for) – it is Kitzbühel, or 'Kitz' as aficionados like to call it, one of the most famous and colourful ski resorts in the world.

Its medieval walled and cobbled streets, clustered gabled houses, arches and buildings with colour-washed facades are a delight; its tea rooms and coffee shops (Praxmair's and Kortshak's are the best known) and their contents delicious, and the whole atmosphere of the place is colourful, full of fun and – perhaps surprisingly – fairly unpretentious.

It is almost as though one of the livelier, more colourful corners of Vienna has been transported to the mountains to enable skiers to enjoy the best of both worlds. They say that about a third of the people who spend their holidays in Kitzbühel never actually ski. In a resort like this, I can almost understand why.

The Kitzbühel area is packed with history. It was settled in prehistoric times, and during the Bronze Age and again in the fifteenth century it was an important copper centre. It became known as 'Chizbuhel' in the twelfth century – named after the family of Chizzo who ruled it. It was also important because it lay on the shortest route between Bavaria and Venice.

The fairy-tale centre of medieval Kitzbühel.

Opposite
Kitzbühel – home of the dreaded Hahnenkamm World Cup downhill race.

Elisabeth Hussey's book *The World's Greatest Ski Holidays* describes how Kitzbühel's skiing history owes a great deal to the Norwegian explorer Fridtjof Nansen. In 1890 he published a book called *On Ski Across Greenland*, explaining how helpful 'ski' could be in reaching inaccessible territory.

The mayor of Kitzbühel read the book and wrote off to Norway to order a pair of skis. When they arrived at the local post office, they were much admired, and the mayor, Franz Reisch set off to try them out. [In spite of their extraordinary length – at 230 centimetres (eight feet!) they were as long as those used today by speed-skiers over the kilometre lancée – he mastered them well enough to achieve a personal ambition and climb the Kitzbühelerhorn.] By 1893 he and his friends had formed the Kitzbühel Ski Association. Luckily one of Reisch's great friends was a photographer. Early photographs show the ski pioneers in tweed jackets, with gaitered legs and single long poles which they used both for balance and for breaking.

By 1900 visitors were already coming to Kitzbühel to learn to ski – among them troops training for mountain warfare. Now, of course, 'Kitz' is famous as an international ski resort and above all, for its stomach-churningly fearsome downhill classic on the Hahnenkamm, the 'Streif', whose initial

Kitzbühel is Austria's most picturesque ski town, and during the height of the season is rather too popular for comfort.

steepness is so frighteningly dramatic when you see it in the flesh that you realize how television cameras foreshorten everything. You might care to ski it after the race. It will still be icy and you realize once and for all what a fearsome run it is – especially when you remember that the professionals go straight down! You don't have to ski it in two minutes at eighty miles per hour. Indeed, your route will no doubt be littered with other would-be Franz Klammers all desperate to tell their friends they have skied it. So even if you wanted to take it quickly, you would probably find it impossible to avoid other skiers.

Even Kitzbühel's lack of height (760 metres; 2,494 feet – or 800 metres if you want to round it up like some tour operators do) is not as serious as it might be; the resort seems to be in a snow pocket and often has snow – including some excellent powder – when it has no right to expect it.

With four main ski areas – Hahnenkamm, Kirchberg-Fleckalm, Kitzbühelerhorn and Jochberg-Pass Thurn (which alone is larger than some entire Austrian resorts) – there are more than 180 kilometres (112 miles) of prepared pistes, which are spread among Kitzbühel, its near neighbour and satellite Kirchberg, and the interlinking ski circus of Aschau, Aurach, Jochberg and Pass Thurn. Helping you to ski them are Kitzbühel's two hundred famous 'Red Devils' ski instructors.

Kitzbühel, right at the western end of the Tyrol, is sandwiched between the striking and beautiful Kitzbühelerhorn (just under 2000 metres, (6,562 feet) with wonderful views and some excellent 'motorway' and off-piste skiing reminiscent of Ischgl) and the Hahnenkamm. Short of skiing the Hahnenkamm itself, including that terrifying first drop, the skiing beneath the Steinbergkogel is among the most challenging in the area, with some quite black sections. There is also challenging skiing at Pass Thurn (open as late as April) under the Resterhohe and Zweitausender chair lifts. Hochetz and Stuchkogel are limited on-piste but good areas for off-piste, with runs down to Oberaurach or Fieberbrunn.

Elsewhere the skiing tends to be just a little on the tame side. Predictably, there are often human traffic jams in the morning as people flock to the Hahnenkamm cable car which travels from 792 metres – 1646 metres (2,600 feet – 5,400 feet) or two-stage chair lift in the centre of the town. From the top there is a sprawling collection of no fewer than fourteen lifts criss-crossing the area and connecting with Ehrenbachhohe, the Steinbergkogel, and Pengelstein.

Kitzbühel's skiing also has some wonderfully Gilbert and Sullivan sounding names such as Bärenbadkogel, Wilde Hag and Giggling!

The queuing first thing in the morning from the town centre at Kitzbühel can verge on the appalling, as can the behaviour of some of the lager louts who help form the queues. One way round this is to make use of the free bus service to the Fleckalmbahn gondola station or the Jochberg and Pass Thurn lifts which tend to be less crowded.

It does not really matter in the end how you get up the mountain. Getting down should be a joy. And just think of all those gooey cakes, hot chocolates and *gemutlichkeit* waiting for you at the end of a wonderful day in Austria's most famous ski resort.

SKI FACTS

RESORT HEIGHT	800 m
RANGE	770 – 1973 m
BLACK RUNS	10
RED RUNS	28
BLUE RUNS	34
TOTAL	72
PISTES	180 km
LIFTS	60
LONGEST RUN	8 km

Kitzbühel

LECH/ZURS

I have always suspected that Lech is another Gstaad – the trendiest of resorts without quite having the skiing to back it up.

I do not mean to damn Lech or Zurs with faint praise. They are both delightful – especially Lech. It is just that their reputation is so glitzy that one half expects the skiing to be out of this world rather than merely part of it. Nearby St Anton wins hands down on the skiing, so why do the smart set make for Lech and its companion resort, Zurs? (Sit down at any restaurant and you are liable to find yourself sitting next to royalty of some description or another. In my case it was Princess Caroline of Monaco, who chatted happily away to me over a goulash soup.)

Probably one of the principal reasons is that it is sheer habit. Lech and Zurs, charming spots that they may be, are and always have been the places in which to be seen. If visitors become bored with the skiing, they can always drive 'next door' and slake their skiing desires on the Herculean slopes of St Anton, with which Lech and Zurs share the Arlberg ski region. (St Anton and its tiny but idyllic satellite, St Christoph are in the Tyrol,

Lech and Zurs are in the province of Vorarlberg.)

Lech is by far the older (fourteenth century), larger and more traditional of the two, and the more 'genuine.' Zurs is pleasant enough – especially for what is essentially a purpose-built resort of sorts. In fact from a distance it looks almost as rustic as Lech. But when you move closer you quickly realize that it is a clever, tasteful subterfuge.

Lech has a higher satellite called, inevitably, Oberlech, which is more important as a meeting place for Lech's beautiful set than for its skiing, although it does add an extra dimension to the ski area.

Its most famous landmark is also its flimsiest: a large red umbrella outside the Sporthotel Petersboden. There is something very pleasant about eating and drinking outside – perhaps even in a flurry of snow – under what in England is usually a symbol of wet, windy and rather miserable weather.

Both Lech and Zurs are somewhat off the beaten track which is one reason the regulars go there.

Austria's most upmarket and expensive ski area is linked with the more serious skiing of St Anton.

Until the end of the last century and later, Lech was often cut off from the outside world for months at a time. And even during the summer, it could only be reached by rough, ready and sometimes quite dangerous mule tracks (even today the Flexenpass can be blocked for long periods).

In the winter of 1895, the then parish priest at Lech caused some amusement when he procured a pair of skis in order to undertake his rounds more easily. The amusement turned to rather more serious thoughts as others began to follow his example, and the first recreational skiers began to arrive in the village. Lech, totally unexpectedly, began to prosper. And has done ever since.

In 1920, Hannes Schneider pioneered the Austrian style of skiing that replaced the old Telemark turns with the 'stem-Christiania' which became the basis of today's technique. He complained that Telemark turns pinched his toes. (Ironically Telemark turns – with certain modern refinements to the original equipment – are now very fashionable again.)

Schneider himself was a pupil in the first ski school at Zurs as a sixteen-year-old in 1906. (There are now six hundred ski instructors working in the Arlberg.)

Austria's first ski tow lift was built in Zurs in 1937. Lech itself followed suit two years later.

At least Lech does not seem to suffer from the 'fat cat' syndrome that resorts such as Courchevel and Zermatt used to display until quite recently. The resort certainly seems genuinely anxious to please. 'More than three thousand people are trying very hard every day to help you to enjoy your holiday' they stress. 'It is very important to us that you feel well here, that you are happy and pleased with our holiday atmosphere, and we are concerned for your safety . . . But nobody is perfect . . !'

The skiing in Zurs is high and all above the tree-line (and therefore can become very cold). They like to make a virtue out of this by boasting that

Lech: more fur coats than ski jackets, but some good skiing for the keen.

there is not a single tree in their entire ski area. It does mean the off-piste is good and also accessible, bearing in mind the recently introduced law in Austria that skiing through the trees near pistes is generally prohibited. There are, however – by way of contrast – plenty of tree-lined runs in Lech's skiing terrain. Some of the best skiing here is reached by the Rufikopf cable car – either back down to Lech or down past the Rufispitze to Zurs. The skiing in Lech tends to be relatively bland and gentle, but there are a few rather sterner runs off the Kriegerhorn, particularly the run down to Zug.

The more difficult skiing is further afield on the unpisted ski routes from the Zuger Hochlicht – Lech's highest point at 2377 metres (7,800 feet) – or down to Zug, a tiny hamlet via Madloch-Joch, linking with a similar run from Zurs.

The best skiing in Zurs is arguably reached from the top of the Trittkopf cable car and from the Zursersee lifts, particularly the off-piste runs down to Zug and Lech. There is another steep unpisted run reached from the Zurs skiing area back to Lech from the top of the Rufikopf cable car.

I remember one particularly delicious off-piste run down to Zurs after a very long walk, sweltering in rolled-up ski-sweater sleeves, to the Muggengrat area. Worth every sweaty yard getting there.

But the classic run down to Zurs is the formidable descent from the north face of St Anton's Valluga. Few people realize that you can ski from St Anton to Zurs – and for reasons which quickly become apparent when you first set eyes on the descent. This can only be attempted with a guide.

From the top of the 'normal' cable car up to the Valluga you take a tiny yellow cable car with room for half a dozen or so people up to the very summit of the Valluga. You are only allowed inside this lift with a guide. Ours was Joe Mellaun, a young man whose task it is to teach other St Anton instructors snowcraft. He inspires utter and total confidence which is just as well, because this run is seriously disturbing. The initial part of the descent is fearsomely steep. The Consumer Association's excellent *Good Skiing Guide* says: 'The descent towards Zurs starts perilously.' I have underlined this sentence in my own copy with a degree of satisfaction.

As you try to follow in the ski tracks of the indomitable Joe, he says: 'You must ski exactly where I ski' and indeed becomes untypically cross when you fail to do so. It soon becomes apparent – as if you did not already realize it – that this is serious skiing. It is better to look neither down at the steep slopes beneath you, nor back up again to see what appears to be the vertical cliff you are half-way down. At last you are down the worst section and the fun begins – acre upon acre of superb powder fields almost all the way down to Zurs.

When you reach Zurs, you feel a little like an astronaut must feel after splash-down – and you almost want people to ask about the bus journey from St Anton just so you can amaze them by saying: 'Well, actually we didn't take the bus. We skied. (Dramatic pause for reaction.)' Disappointingly, no one asks.

I think this run is probably the most challenging I have ever skied. Joe (who recently teamed up with a friend to win the World Powder 8 Championships in America) has taken me down it three times so far and I cannot wait to do it again.

The man is pure magic. He makes you feel you could ski down Everest – as long as he leads the way. He and the St Anton ski area together make a formidably exciting combination.

SKI FACTS		
RESORT HEIGHT	Lech 1450 m	
	Zurs 1720 m	
RANGE	1445 – 2450 m	
BLACK RUNS	8	
RED RUNS	20	
BLUE RUNS	19	
TOTAL	47	
PISTES	100 km	
LIFTS	32	

SAALBACH/ HINTERGLEMM

Ski resorts are like lovers – one should never forget old flames or how much they meant to you at the time – and perhaps still do. For a while Saalbach/Hinterglemm, less than two hours from Salzburg airport in the sun-kissed Glemm Valley, was my best love. Not that I had the area to myself. The twin resorts comprise the most frequently visited holiday centre in Austria after the capital, Vienna, and are among the most popular with the Austrians themselves.

Between them, Saalbach and Hinterglemm have a little of everything – rustic charm, some good intermediate skiing, bright but not too boisterous a nightlife, efficient, well-thought-out lifts, and altogether a most pleasing atmosphere for any ski resort. Even though the resorts are no longer my first choice, I have not forgotten the magic of the times when – almost like one's first serious love affair – I discovered what skiing was really all about. It was in Saalbach/Hinterglemm – in a single day of rapturous skiing – that I stopped being a beginner and joined the heady world of the intermediate.

Between them, these two resorts, just four kilometres apart (and closing) in Salzburgerland's Kitzbühel Alps, have a 'Ski Circus' of more than 180 kilometres (112 miles) of marked pistes served by around sixty lifts. You can enter the 'circus' from either village and ski it methodically, either clockwise or anti-clockwise, which takes a lot of careful planning by the lift companies.

Most of the ribbon development in the valley which has taken place as the lift systems have grown is recent, but the resorts have managed to avoid most of the mistakes made by post-war architects elsewhere in the Alps. The two main centres are busy and often crowded. They are crammed with hotels, pensions and apartments, but they are low-rise and give the impression of being older than they are.

Most of the skiing is intermediate, with long, uncomplicated runs which are a joy to someone who has finally cracked the secret of proper skiing and wants to practise his or her new skills without encountering anything too threatening.

The valley runs from west to east, with the pistes ranged mainly along both sides. This means that a great deal of the skiing is south-facing. In warm weather, these slopes are best skied after the sun has had time to soften them, but they can become slushy by mid-afternoon.

The skiing links up with the neighbouring resort of Leogang, which lies in a parallel valley to the north. Also close by is the picturesque resort of Zell am See, set by the beautiful Zellersee lake and not far from Kaprun and the exciting Kitzsteinhorn, Austria's best summer ski area.

Among the more exciting tests in this somewhat bland area are the runs down to both villages from the 2020-metre (6,627-foot) Schattberg (the key link between the two resorts, with its cable car). From the Schattberg a fine, north-facing black run returns to the road opposite the lift station. It begins with a fairly easy right-hand sweep around the mountain, has a short, sharp stretch through the trees half-way down, and runs out in what is often a sea of large moguls. None of it would be too difficult for an adventurous intermediate, however. Behind the Schattberg there is an open, treeless area of fairly easy skiing, with broad, undemanding pistes. But you can ignore these and

Austria's twin resorts are firm favourites with the British.

SKI FACTS

RESORT HEIGHT	1003 m
RANGE	1003 – 2020 m
BLACK RUNS	7
RED RUNS	32
BLUE RUNS	24
TOTAL	63
PISTES	180 km
LIFTS	57
LONGEST RUN	7 km

head off down a red run towards the Limberg-Hochalm. The red runs becomes a blue trail, winding through the forest to Jausernalm and Vorderglemm, its last stages sometimes tricky with ice.

From there, unless you return to Saalbach by bus, you must take the cable car and ski the excellent, fast red run beneath that, or take the subsequent lift to the Wildenkarkogel. That gives you two options: to return to Saalbach or turn east to the foot of the lift to the Schönleitenhutte and work your way via Mulda to the Kleine Asitz where you start the long cruise down to Leogang. *En route* there is a pleasant little powder bowl which in good conditions would be ideally suited to skiers just learning off-piste technique.

The descent to Leogang begins with a wonderful boulevard of a blue, ideal for perfecting linked turns, but the runs further down towards the village can be very icy. On the run back from Leogang to Saalbach, there is nothing in the least demanding – just a series of gentle ups and downs and, at one point, usually a fair bit of poling. If you turn *right* from the Schattberg, you take a short ridge and swing into a broad gulley to the foot of the Westgipfel lift. This run is marked black, though it only just qualifies, but the snow on the latter part of it is often in good condition.

The Westgipfel lift tends to be a cold ride, but it is worth it. From its top station you can take a marvellous red run down to Hinterglemm. Perhaps a quarter of the way down the prepared piste swings right, but you can take an unpisted ski trail if you carry on in a traverse. The ski trail is not difficult, but allows a range of options through the trees and can be great fun in the right conditions.

Whichever option you take, you end up back on the piste for the lower section of the run, a very fine red, and eventually swing right for the Hinterglemm baby slopes or left for the lifts to the Zwölfer. Again, because this is a relatively low lift complex, the lowest reaches of this descent can be worn and difficult.

Beneath the Zwölfer there are two chairs to the Winklerhof with a choice of three descents, two red and one blue. Again, the reds are prone to ice, but there is now artificial snow-making equipment on both. Above that there are two more chair lifts, opening a number of further options. Straight back

down gives you an easy red and a very tricky little black run, short but often heavily mogulled and convex so that, if you catch an edge, you may be unlucky enough to fall a considerable distance. Turn left and you come to the pleasant, sunny, Seekar area, with red and blue intermediate runs of no special challenge.

Turn right, however, and you encounter a slope which matches most in the Alps for difficulty. This is the so-called Zwolfer Nord, a black, unpisted ski trail which starts fairly innocuously but plunges into an extremely steep mogul field. Cross the road at its foot and you can take a chair to the Hochalm, where there is a restaurant and a further choice of lifts opening up a fine selection of red, intermediate runs, which though not difficult are generally very enjoyable. From there you can work your way back to Hinterglemm via a network of lifts, probably emerging by the Reiterkogel lift.

Most of the area's runs are short by the standards of the big circuses in the French Alps, and I have not been shown any outstanding powder ski possibilities, but much of the skiing is extremely pleasant, and there is a good range of mountain restaurants.

Saalbach probably has the tougher skiing of the two: The four-kilometre (2½-mile) Nord descent to the village below the cable car is a healthy black, with a vertical descent of 1000 metres (3,280 feet); the run to Hinterglemm is a red. One of Hinterglemm's better and most difficult runs is the Zwolferkogel (1984 metres; 6,510 feet) World Cup run. There is an enjoyable seven-kilometre (4½-mile) run from the top of the cable car down to the Zell am See Road which even modest skiers would cope with.

Although their snow record is good, Saalbach/Hinterglemm have been quicker than many Austrian resorts to bring in snow cannons to supplement the natural supplies with artificial snow, particularly on the sunny Bernkogel and Kohlmais slopes.

Recent additions to the lift system include a twelve-person cable car from Vorderglemm to Hochwartalm.

My enduring memory of Saalbach-Hinterglemm is Tea Dancing at a firelit bar, still – like everyone else – wearing my skiing boots. It is very much that kind of place both as a ski resort and holiday centre: lots of *gemutlichkeit* and good cheer.

ST ANTON/
St Christoph

If Walt Disney had been commissioned to design a ski resort, he would surely have been well-satisfied with St Anton, the Tyrolean titan nestling (if such a stretched-out resort can nestle) at 1304 metres (4,250 feet) in Austria's superb and distinctive Arlberg region.

St Anton towers peak and shoulders above the rest of Austrian resorts. It is magnificent, majestic and awe-inspiring both to behold and to ski.

Like other giants, such as Val d'Isere, Jackson Hole, and Verbier, it is such a swashbuckling, thoroughbred ski resort that it is almost too good to be true. If it has a snag – again like Jackson Hole – it is almost too machismo in spirit, thus risking terrifying the more timid and inexperienced skiers

even before they have nervously selected their 170s!

But to continue the Wyoming analogy for a moment – St Anton too has its milder mountain (the Gampberg, 2408 metres (7,900 feet), served by the Rendl gondola) just as Jackson has its Apres Vous peak. No skier of any ability should be put off, but it has to be said that St Anton is a resort which benefits advanced and intermediate skiers much more than beginners.

The first time you visit St Anton – and even the second and third time – the extent of the skiing is bewildering. There are 200 kilometres (125 miles) of pistes (twelve blue runs, twenty-one reds and seven blacks) in St Anton, but if you take the Arlberg region (adding neighbouring Zurs and

Before I left St Anton, I bought a small cup and set a slalom on the nursery slopes for the boys of the village, the first modern slalom set in Austria. The boys were delighted with this unknown type of race. I suggested to Schneider that a cup, to be called the Arlberg-Kandahar, should be presented by the Kandahar Club (Mürren) for competitions in the Arlberg.

When the Nazis occupied Austria and arrested Schneider, they very much wanted to keep the 'A-K' race going. Lunn refused to co-operate unless Schneider was released. 'You can't stop us calling the race the Arlberg-Kandahar' said the Nazi Buergermeister defiantly. To which Lunn replied: 'And the Jockey Club could not prevent you holding a donkey race in St Anton and calling it The Derby!' When Schneider was finally allowed to leave for America, Lunn still refused to co-operate. 'But you promised!' said the Germans. 'I said I would not bring back that Arlberg-Kandahar unless you let Schneider go' said Lunn. 'That was our first condition. The second is that you get rid of Hitler.'

Today, from the Valluga and the Kapall areas, red runs galore – and a few fierce blacks – fan out in all directions. An alternative route up the Valluga – although it actually falls short of the cable car top station – is the extraordinary Arlen Sattel chair lift up the Schindlerspitze, which has stunning and dramatic terrain and scenery both on the way up and again as you arrive, dangling in space among jagged mountain tops, fearsome and barely skiable (by true experts only) couloirs and, from the top, as you go up and over a precipitous rock face, a truly remarkable panoramic view.

From the Vallugabahn (cable car) itself, it is possible for expert skiers with a guide to go even higher to the very top of the Vullugagrat in a tiny yellow cable car and ski an extreme run down to

Lech from the nearby province of Vorarlberg) as a whole, there are a total of seventy red runs, which makes it a true skier's paradise, unlike so many lesser resorts which merely *claim* to be.

The introduction of artificial snow-making machines on the lower slopes means that St Anton's snow record – already excellent – is now almost infallible.

The pivotal mountain in St Anton's ski area is the famous Valluga (2811 metres; 9,222 feet) and the Kapall area nearby (2326 metres; 7,630 feet) from which the famous Arlberg-Kandahar race starts. It was launched in 1928 by Sir Arnold Lunn when he was a guest of Hannes Schneider. Lunn recalls in his book *Kandahar Story*:

The ultimate: perfect helicopter-skiing conditions far from the madding lift queues.

Previous page
Snug in the snow – St Christoph, a tiny gem of a ski resort and a secret haunt of the Prince and Princess of Wales.

Zurs through some excellent powder fields. (See chapter on Lech and Zurs.)

St Anton is famed for its mogul fields, and among the more dramatic of these are the runs at Mattun, Schindlergrat and Schongraben.

As well as its links (by ski bus) with Lech and Zurs, St Anton, the star of the Arlberg system, has a minuscule 'moon', St Christoph at 1800 metres (5,900 feet) concealed close by, and reached via St Anton's Galzig area (first reached on skis in the winter of 1899).

This tiniest of ski resorts – a handful of buildings cocooned in deep snow like a plate of profiteroles with too much cream – has a fairy-tale quality unrepeated anywhere in Austria. It is no light-weight, however. One of the country's principal government run schools for training ski instuctors is based here, and in 1901, the prestigious Arlberg Ski Club, which would in future organize many of the famous local ski races, was formed at the tiny village's focal point, the Hospiz Hotel.

Built on the fourteenth-century site of the original Hospiz (which recently celebrated its five hundredth anniversary) its monks once provided shelter and food for travellers caught in fierce snow storms as they struggled over the ancient Arlberg Pass, a vital trade and military route across the Alps. Occasionally more was at stake – without assistance, travellers sometimes perished.

The pass has a touch of the Utah/Wyoming weather pattern built into its meteorological system: it can be bathed in brilliant sunshine one minute and enveloped in anything from chilling mists to violent snow storms the next. It is more than usually prone to avalanches, rock falls and landslides.

The Arlberg not only marks the boundary between the Tyrol and Vorarlberg. It is also a watershed between the rivers Inn and Danube and the Black Sea on one side, and the Ill, Rhine and North Sea on the other.

But back to the Hospiz Hotel where the owner, Adi Werner, claims to have the best wine cellers in Austria – one of which is concealed beneath the hamlet's picturesque church. Having sampled some of his better bottles – including an immac-

Ski-touring: the hard way up. This is how they used to do it before ski lifts – and helicopters.

ulate Chateau Palmer 1961, I cannot dispute this. Some of the most knowledgeable wine experts from Europe gather here once a year for a very exclusive tasting session. Some of the wines they open date back to Napoleonic times. Even when consumed, the bottles are well worth preserving, and the best ones end up on display in a special show case.

It is a wonderful, if expensive, location for honeymoon couples and rich folk who want to be able to enjoy the quiet and exclusive intimacy of a luxury hotel in an idyllic mountain village, while at the same time being able to ski in one of the most vast and exhilarating ski resorts in the world. (The Prince and Princess of Wales have made more than one secret visit.)

If guests wish to inject even further fantasy into their visit, they could travel home on the Venice–Simplon Orient Express, which stops at St Anton. When I experienced this rare treat the journey lived up to all expectations as the express curled its way through the snowy dusk of the mountains. I especially enjoyed the romance and excitement of having my excellent meal accompanied by a singer/pianist whose tinkling melodies echoed through the dining car above the clickety-clack of the wheels, and in spite of the thundering as we journeyed the ten kilometres (six miles) through the Arlberg tunnel. (This was built in an astonishing feat of engineering between 1879 and 1883.) After some wonderfully exhilarating helicopter skiing in St Anton, the journey was almost too much for the senses!

St Anton was quicker off the mark than many places in developing its skiing. Lessons were being held on the slopes at St Anton and St Christoph as long ago as 1902. By 1907, Hannes Schneider, who was born in nearby Stuben (see chapter on Lech and Zurs) was starting to give particular attention to guests from abroad, and in 1912 he founded his famous Arlberg Ski School. His technique is still taught today, although some – especially the French – openly criticize the Austrian style for its studied inflexibility.

Personally I admire both the French and Austrian way of skiing, and I am not trying to be diplomatic. It would be boring if every nation practised the same style. The French, in my view, should relish 'la difference' although the choice can confuse beginners.

Whatever the style, however, skiing was about to become big business in the Arlberg. The Galzig cable-way started operating in 1937, its cabins then carrying just 210 people an hour up the mountain. After the Second World War the St Christoph cable car arrived in 1952, followed by the Valluga and Schindler cable cars (1954/55), the Arlberg-Kandahar (1972), Rendl (1974) and Schindlergrat (1981).

St Anton is almost the antithesis of the conventional idea of the quintessential Austrian ski village. This is partly due to its size, although Kitzbühel is large too but it has managed to retain the basic traditional atmosphere.

St Anton, in spite of its car-free and care-free centre and charm of a different kind, is a rather boisterous, international town epitomized perhaps by its infamous Krazy Kangaruh bar where skiers congregate on their last run down and – if sufficiently inebriated or otherwise inspired – jump on skis from the verandah. This practice is frowned upon by the authorities, but is difficult to police.

You can, however, understand their exuberance. St Anton and its skiing does get to you. A leap off the Krazy Kangaruh is simply a tribute to the exciting razzmatazz of the place.

SKI FACTS	
RESORT HEIGHT	1304 m
RANGE	1304 – 2811 m
BLACK RUNS	7
RED RUNS	21
BLUE RUNS	12
TOTAL	40
PISTES	200 km
LIFTS	31
LONGEST RUN	8 km

ALPE D'HUEZ

This wonderful, sunny, all-round resort, high above the Romanche Valley, with its superb off-piste skiing and some of the latest and fastest uphill transport has only started to explode in the British consciousness in the last few years.

There has been skiing in this part of the Dauphine region for almost a century, and one of the first lifts in the French Alps, the Teleski de l'Eclose was built here in 1936.

But just as the Austrians kept quiet about Ischgl, the canny French tried to keep Alpe d'Huez for themselves. In a French poll recently, the French put the resort in their top five. It was only after the Grenoble Olympics that one of France's best-kept skiing secrets leaked out to the rest of Europe. The leak now threatens to turn into an avalanche. I only discovered Alpe d'Huez myself in 1988, though I had been hearing good things about it for some time. They were all true.

The resort (purpose-built, but far from ugly) is perched at 1860 metres (6,102 feet), in a sun-trap, on a vast, bowl-shaped ledge above Bourg d'Oisans. When the sun comes out, the whole place basks in

Alpe d'Huez: not just a skier's paradise.

Right
The futuristic church at dusk.

it for almost the entire day. Indeed, there is a local saying: 'When it's not sunny in Alpe d'Huez – it must be night time.'

The skiing is excellent for all standards. You simply cannot go wrong. And for off-piste fanatics, one of the truly great runs sweeps down from the south-west face of the Pic Blanc (3330 metres; 10,925 feet) through a couloir that a strong intermediate skier could cope with, and then down, gloriously down, to the village again. There is also some superb powder skiing on the way down to the new resort of Oz en Oisans, which opened in 1987/88. Altogether there are seven ski areas, linked by some of the most modern lifts in Europe.

There are more than eighty lifts giving access to 220 kilometres (136 miles) of pistes. The resort of Vaujany, next to Oz, was due to open up after being linked with Alpe d'Huez's ski area, but tragically the connecting cable car – one of the largest in the world – crashed during final tests in the winter of 1988/89, killing the eight mechanics on board. In spite of this terrible setback, the new link will no doubt be in operation soon.

Of Alpe d'Huez's eighty-nine runs, eleven are black, twenty-two red, thirty are blue and thirty-three green. The skiing is in three main areas: Grandes Rousses, Signal and Signal de l'Homme. From the Pic Blanc (3330 metres; 10,925 feet) you can ski down the Glacier de Sarenne (no crevasses) which offers some of Europe's classic black descents as well as sensational scenery – or you can approach the zenith of recreational skiing by taking a guide and trying some of the exceptional off-piste runs.

On piste, La Sarenne, a sixteen-kilometre (ten-mile) descent, is claimed to be Europe's longest black run. La Combe du Loup is as good as any black I have encountered, and reminded me of an even steeper version of the Swiss 'wall' at Avoriaz. The Chateau-Noir variant is even tougher – about as black as a run can become before being classified as off-piste.

'If it's not sunny it must be night-time'.

The tough Tunnel run starts as a steep mogul slope beneath the cable car until skiers veer off through a tunnel bored in the rock and, as they blink in the daylight at the other end, they are presented with a descent which is even steeper and more bumpy.

But it is from the south-west face of the Pic Blanc itself that you can experience skiing at something approaching its outer limits. A number of very long off-piste runs start here. The initial descent is spectacular, very steep and should only be undertaken by genuine experts with a guide.

But advanced intermediates can easily tackle the bulk of these runs simply by bypassing the initial super-expert terrain and joining the runs a little further down. There is still plenty of mileage left. So much, in fact, that even the fittest skiers will start to wilt a little long before they are back in the village.

For those who want fast, easy but less-dramatic skiing, the Signal area provides a number of long, sweeping 'motorway' runs ending in the satellite resort of Villard-Reculas. Although the main skiing area is just north of the village, this is linked through the Telecentre bucket lift with several other areas. The transport up to the Grandes Rousses area is by ultra-modern twenty-five-person gondolas. The final leg up to Pic Blanc is by cable car.

There is more than enough skiing for everyone at Alpe d'Huez, but if you want a change of scene for a day, the resort of Les Deux Alpes is only forty minutes away across the valley, and a day's skiing here is included on the Alpe d'Huez lift pass should you want it. If you are really impatient to get there, you can reach it by helicopter in five minutes for around £40 return. Helicopter skiing as such is banned in France, so it is not possible to be transported to powder skiing. However there is a way round this problem. If you can find your own way to good off-piste runs (preferably with a guide); it is possible to arrange for a helicopter to pick you up at the *bottom* of the run.

Further afield, over the stunningly beautiful Col de Lautaret is the highly enjoyable and immensely skiable collection of villages known jointly as Serre Chevalier. This is a great day out for skiers who enjoy non-stop 'red-arrow' cruising on well-groomed pistes linking several small resorts. There is one spectacular part of the circuit where huge drops open up on both sides of you and you seem to be skiing on a knife-edge ridge on top of the world. The views are stunning and heady and you feel very insignificant in the general scheme of things.

Serre Chevalier is also famous for its excellent and abundant powder fields. Again, an optional day here is included in your pass. This also applies to Puy St Vincent and the Milky Way, a wonderfully scenic outing from Montgenèvre deep into Italy and back for intermediates. You can reach a number of Italian resorts, but the usual destination is Sauze d'Oulx, somewhat unkindly dubbed 'Benidorm on Ice.'

But you can see why, and I would sooner pay a flying visit than stay there; it is fun to visit if only because it is also fun to ski it and then leave. Especially if you are heading back to such an effervescent and dynamic ski resort as Alpe d'Huez.

SKI FACTS

RESORT HEIGHT	1860 m
RANGE	up to 3350 m
BLACK RUNS	11
RED RUNS	22
BLUE RUNS	30
GREEN RUNS	33
TOTAL	96
PISTES	230 km
LIFTS	41
LONGEST RUN	16 km

alpe d'huez

ARGENTIERE

Foolish but fun! How not to ski off the top of Grands Montets.

Opposite
Skiing through Argentière's dramatic glacial terrain.

Take a cliff or two from Jackson Hole, a generous slice of La Grâve, a large measure of Val d'Isère, mix with plenty of panache and cool till ready to serve. Add several feet of powder snow and several large chunks of ice. Ski. Argentière, the skier's ski resort, will bring *you* to the boil.

This unsophisticated and old world village with its dramatic and superb skiing probably suffers a little from being in the shadow – indeed, actually *part* of – France's most celebrated climbing centre, Chamonix. Were it somewhere else – instead of a mere seven kilometres (four miles) away – it would be able to bask in its own glory rather than risk being thought of as just a satellite of somewhere much more famous.

Some skiers are so preoccupied with Chamonix that they do not even bother to visit Argentière. An enormous mistake. It has most of Chamonix's best skiing. It is the fabulous and unusually challenging and beautiful off-piste skiing that attracts the real *cognoscenti* to Argentière, with some stupendous

scenery thrown in. The runs here are the most advanced and demanding in the area – wonderfully long and challenging and in good conditions arguably the best in Europe.

The focul point is the Grands Montets area where queuing for the cable car, a notorious bottleneck, has been relieved to a certain extent by the construction of a new lift running parallel with it up towards the half-way station at Croix de Lognan. And an excellent new skiing area has been opened up at La Pendant. Argentière's skiing – over a huge area – is simply magnificent on and off-piste, with some of the best powder skiing anywhere.

The scenery is remarkable, largely because of the spectacular seracs and associated glacial formations. These extraordinary ice formations formed long, long ago by the debris of criss-crossing glaciers on the move give the scenery an almost dream-like quality.

With a guide – absolutely essential off-piste because of crevasse and avalanche danger – you can actually ski around and even through some of them

to enjoy skiing in a near-fantasy world rarely encountered in ski resorts.

Apart from the seracs and moraine, there are spectacular rock formations lining some of the off-piste gulleys which give the runs a different perspective, extra drama, and enhance the skiing. Off-piste runs seem much more exciting with outcrops of rock and the odd cliff and aquamarine ice walls to enhance the thrills.

The mountainside above Lognan is criss-crossed with ridges of ice and rock, bowls, moguls, gulleys and chutes, all above the tree-line. On the way down the Glacier d'Argentière you can even ski over a large frozen waterfall. One of today's theme park designers could never have organized anything like it – and the whole breathtaking scene is of course perfectly natural.

Most keen skiers regard the Pas de Chèvre (Goat's Hop) as the toughest and most exhilarating run in Argentière, and one of the most challenging off-piste descents in Europe. It sweeps down from the Grands Montets and links up with the celebrated Vallée Blanche run to Chamonix. Being south-facing there is a strong risk of avalanches and the run is often unskiable and closed.

I was supremely fortunate to be able to ski it during my last-but-one visit, not realizing my luck at the time. In bad conditions it can take an eternity to get down, and a guide is essential. Bladon Lines go as far as saying that the skiing in Argentière is 'the next best thing to helicopter skiing in the Canadian Rockies.' Having tried both I would agree with them.

Argentière itself is virtually a one-street town, but no less quaint for that, although the overall appearance is somewhat marred by some rather ugly apartment blocks which are something of an eyesore. Some of the buildings, however, date back to the eighteenth century. In one of its handful of bars – the Savoie – you can find your beer being served in huge glass boots.

Argentière is not really a place for beginners. Almost every run has a considerable degree of difficulty. The resort is at 1250 metres (4,100 feet), with skiing up to 3300 metres (10,826 feet), so the vertical drop is more than 2000 metres (6,560 feet).

Chardonnay – one of Argentière's most spectacular landmarks.

This produces some wonderfully exciting runs. It is very much a skier's – or even a 'ski bum's' – ski resort, with its own band of dedicated aficionados, who rate it as one of the best and most beautiful off-piste resorts in Europe. Some would go further and say the best in the world.

One of the few snags is the weather, which can be sullen, murky and threatening in the extreme. The Chamonix Valley is renowned for its unpredictable weather patterns and you need a degree of luck to be there at the right time – or not to be there at the wrong one.

I last skied Argentière early in the winter of 1988/89, when many resorts were suffering from yet another crisis over snow conditions. The lower third and top third of the Grands Montets were closed. And yet I enjoyed some of the best skiing I have ever experienced, especially in the Lavancher area. We were skiing areas that perhaps we might not have thought about had there been the normal amount of snow 'on top.' We were, one could say, skiing Argentière's 'reserve' slopes. To be able to get such magnificent skiing while half the resort was closed down speaks volumes for Argentière.

SKI FACTS

RESORT HEIGHT	1230 m
RANGE	1230 – 3300 m
BLACK RUNS	4
RED RUNS	8
BLUE RUNS	6
GREEN RUNS	2
TOTAL	20
PISTES	100 km
LIFTS	14

AVORIAZ

Purpose built with a vengeance – you either like Avoriaz or you hate it. Loving it is difficult.

Avoriaz, with its craggy splendour, is the jewel and pivotal resort in the crown of a huge circuit of ski resorts between Lake Geneva and Mont Blanc known collectively as the Portes du Soleil (Gateway to the Sun).

Possibly the most popular French resort among British skiers apart from Flaine, it sits at 1800 metres (5,905 feet) overlooking the Morzine Valley. While the skiing potential is huge – the circuit's 360 miles of pistes makes it arguably the biggest linked area of its kind in the world – not everyone appreciates the space-age purpose-built architecture of Avoriaz. And it has to be said, it does suffer from a failing that is not uncommon in such resorts: some of the apartments are cramped. This is partly because the French have an annoying habit of cramming more people into their apartments than the Swiss.

As far as the architecture is concerned, I think Avoriaz is one of the more attractive of the purpose-built ski resorts (its critics would no doubt regard that as a contradiction in terms). Although much of the building was constructed with concrete, it is often quite skilfully disguised as cedar wood. In many cases it really *is* wood – or at least the facade is.

It can be a very romantic or difficult place to get to depending on your point of view and the hour at which you arrive. It is impossible to reach the resort by road in the winter. You must disembark from your coach and complete your journey on one of the many horse-drawn sleigh-vehicles, or even on a snowcat. If you happen to arrive during a blizzard or at night, or possibly both, this can be a somewhat stressful experience.

The skiing potential from Avoriaz is almost limitless. Apart from being one of France's most outstanding resorts in its own right, with some spectacular, rocky-mountain-style scenery, Avoriaz (the Swiss pronounce the Z, the French do not) is the gateway to what is sometimes known as '*le ski sans frontières*' – which means you can get to fourteen other resorts, some in France and others across the Swiss border, without needing a passport. (There are stories in circulation about the occasional skier being asked to produce a passport, but I have never been able to satisfy myself that this has every really happened.)

Among the resorts to which you have access are Champéry, Torgon, Les Crosets, Morgins and Champoussin on the Swiss side and Châtel, Morzine, Les Gets and Abondance in France. The Portes du Soleil lift pass covers more than 220 lifts.

There is also a rather splendid little resort called St Jean d'Aulps which is technically part of the Portes du Soleil, but cut off from the rest of the circuit so that you have to reach it by bus. It is well worth it for a day out, although with so much and such varied skiing on offer *without* taking your skis off, relatively few people bother.

The Portes du Soleil circuit is a tremendously rewarding experience for any skier. It almost does not matter where exactly you wander. One of the few critical decisions is perhaps whether to ski the circuit clockwise or anti-clockwise.

Between Avoriaz and Les Crosets is the Chevanette, one of the most famous descents in the Alps. This is commonly known as the 'Swiss Wall', or to be even more melodramatic, not to say sexist, 'The Widow Maker'. It is indeed one of the biggest and most formidable-looking runs in the Alps, but is not actually quite as steep as it looks. Nevertheless, it is a wonderful challenge for any strong intermediate and certainly no push-over even for the more advanced skier.

The first time you ski it, there is certainly a major sense of achievement – especially if by some fluke you manage to ski it without falling. It is better if you can, because depending on the conditions, a fall can bring you careering the whole way down to the bottom – not to mention the risk to any other skier who happens to be unlucky enough to be in your path. This is usually a humbling and even painful experience, although contrary to local mythology, it is rarely fatal. Apart from the Wall, there are another twenty-one black runs in the Portes du Soleil.

The skiing in Avoriaz itself, with more than thirty lifts, goes as high as 2274 metres (7,700 feet) and is divided into several areas: Le Plateau, which has most of the easiest runs; Les Hauts Forts (a mixture of easy and quite difficult, including the World Cup Downhill course); and the wide-open pistes of Chavanette from the top of which, on a really clear day, you can see the distant Matterhorn.

Then there are number of areas like Les Marmottes and Les Prodains below Avoriaz, which highlight one of the few major snags about the resort: at the end of the day it is not unusual to find yourself adrift way below where you want to get to and having to catch a lift back to the resort again.

Among the local black runs in Avoriaz itself, Les Crozats and Intrets are wothy of special mention.

Even without its fellow resorts in the Portes du Soleil circuit, Avoriaz would be one of Europe's better ski areas. With them, it is something very special indeed. It is summed up poetically by Sally Nesbitt, the area's public relations representative. She is, after all, the actress daughter of Lord Hunt of Everest, so she probably has a deeper understanding of mountains and their mystical qualities than many.

As Summer closes its gates and mountain ash gleams bronzed and scarlet amongst the pine, the first dusting of snow on the Dents du Midi brings thoughts of the coming season, of crisp white mornings, cold fingers and our winter visitors.

Tantalizing thoughts indeed.

SKI FACTS

RESORT HEIGHT	1800 m
RANGE	1600 – 2274 m
BLACK RUNS	4
RED RUNS	9
BLUE RUNS	9
GREEN RUNS	5
TOTAL	27
LIFTS	30+
LONGEST RUN	6 km

CHAMONIX

When the sky is azure and Mont Blanc juts out into it with its huge white canopy basking in the sun, Chamonix, which sits as if in worship at its foot can be a dramatically stirring sight. But on a cold grey day an overwhelming, almost morosely powerful atmosphere can assault your senses even before you reach this famous climbing town.

There is something strange about these particular mountains, with their jagged, spiky peaks and as often as not, the Chamonix weather, which many people including myself find strangely unsettling. Chamonix, dominated by the giant presence of Europe's highest mountain (there is a higher one in White Russia) and the atmosphere that accompanies it, demands respect – and usually gets it. It is a dangerous place to treat flippantly, either on skis or on the end of a climbing rope. Long ago Chamonix was under 1000 metres (3,400 feet) of ice. A chilling frisson seems to remain to this day. Even the official *Focus on Chamonix* guide-book speaks of 'a feeling of being completely absorbed within it, *of no longer being able to escape.*'

At 1000 metres (3,400 feet), Chamonix, with its narrow, hemmed-in, almost claustrophobic streets, pavement cafes and chic boutiques is traditionally and intrinsically more of a mountain town, but the skiing has grown steadily in importance during the last decade or so. But in the beginning it was as a centre for climbing, skating and lugeing that Chamonix was principally known.

In the early days, the only way to reach 'Chamouni' was in a charabanc drawn by horses or mules. The bridges were so narrow that passengers sometimes had to carry the cart themselves. Eventually Napoleon III promised to build them a new road.

A young English traveller, William Windham – who climbed Montenvers with a companion called Pocock – was bringing tourists to the Mer de Glace, that great 'sea of ice' which hangs almost threaten-

The mountain sentinels around the historic climbing town of Chamonix.

ingly near the town, as long ago as 1741. But mountains were not the only attraction. Another was to watch ladies climbing into coaches in 'voluminous crinolines' which were likened by the locals to the 'ascension of balloons!'

It was to Chamonix that Henry Lunn, the pioneer tour operator, brought his first package holiday, escorting forty-five winter sports' enthusiasts in the winter of 1898. They even had the opportunity for an outing on 'ski': six pairs of wooden skis were made available for the occasion. According to legend, they were even given an 'instructor' who, when asked if it were feasible to execute a turn on skis, is supposed to have replied: 'I have heard that with great effort it is possible – but I have never tried it.'

Skis in those days were described as 'two selected pieces of wood: ash and hickory which are carved into listels. The planks are 10 centimetres wide, between three and four centimetres thick, and vary in length between 1.80 and 2.40 metres.'

In 1924, when Chamonix hosted the first winter Olympics in history, downhill skiing was not on the agenda. In those days to ski meant jumping and cross-country. But in 1937 the first official World Championships were held here and by the outbreak of the Second World War, skiing had accomplished a serious grip on the resort. Skating and lugeing had been relegated to pastimes of minor interest and therefore of minor financial importance.

Today there are more that 500 kilometres (310 miles) of skiing in the region, with more than 135 lifts spread over half a dozen basic areas which are linked by a bus service. There is also access on the same lift pass to other resorts such as the traditional and fashionable resort of Megève, Les Contamines and St Gervais. Le Brévent is the only major ski area directly accessible from the town.

The skiing is mainly for intermediates and the more expert. As at Val d'Isère, a red run here could well be a black somewhere else. With skiing as high as 3840 metres (12,600 feet), Chamonix has a wonderful vertical drop.

The most famous descent in Chamonix, and indeed probably in Europe, is the Vallée Blanche, reached from a spectacular two-stage cable-car journey soaring up to the Aiguille du Midi. From the top, it is necessary to clutch two ropes, carrying your skis, and negotiate a long narrow ridge of snow. Over to the left, were you foolish enough to go the wrong way (at least two people have done so) is an invariably fatal drop of more than 3000 metres

Moonscape – high on the powder fields above Chamonix.

(9,840 feet). If you ski the Vallée Blanche out of season – as I did last January – the ropes have not yet been put in place.

You and your companions must be roped up to your guide. Because of the unusual lack of snow at that time, our guide, Giles Claret-Tournier, took us down a dramatic route which turned out to be a truly great adventure. It is the only time I can remember a descent being improved by lack of snow. Many of the huge slabs of ice and seracs that you normally ski straight over when conditions are normal were exposed. In between skiing the most wonderful and unexpected powder, we were roped up again on two occasions to enable Claret-Tournier to lower us over slightly difficult ice walls. Our breathtaking descent was enhanced by the dramatic ice-riddled scenery and superb weather.

For strong beginners and improving intermediates, the standard eighteen-kilometre (eleven-mile) 'tourist route' through Geant and Tacul glaciers and down the Mer de Glace should be a dramatic and exciting watershed. For us – equipped with ice axes, ropes and crampons – it was sensational.

The route is long and frequently (depending on snow conditions) arduous, with very real dangers from crevasses. A guide is essential. Ours was continually testing the snow ahead for signs of those yawning ice caverns that *were* still hidden by snow. The Vallée Blanche is just about as extreme and character-forming as a classic off-piste descent can be without being classified out of hand as 'expert only'. It could almost have been designed specifically as a final test for a mature fledgling about to soar into the heavens on its first real flight.

Stuart Nimmo, a television producer and former TVS colleague who flew over the Vallée Blanche in a helicopter just before Christmas 1988 when an even greater lack of snow revealed the glacier in all its glory, found it a stunning and chilling experience. 'It was like visiting heaven and hell at the same time' he said. 'You just don't realize what you're skiing over. I had no idea what the Vallée Blanche really was until I saw it without snow. It's a huge sea of smashed ice. Some chunks are as big as cathedrals. It was quite astonishing.' Little did I know that I would have the chance of skiing down it in similar conditions so soon after his visit.

The Mer de Glace is between 700 and 1950 metres wide (2,300 – 6,400 feet). It is the second longest glacier in the Alps after the Aletsch at the top of the Jungfraujoch above Wengen. In the winter of 1825/26, the Mer de Glace reached its most significant and disturbing advance when its forty-metre (130-foot) high wall threatened the village of Les Bois, which had to be evacuated. Since then, the glacier has been on the retreat. Even so, the ice is about 240 metres (790 feet) thick, and downstream of the Seracs du Geant, the thickness reaches 400 metres (1,300 feet).

The then staggering idea of building a cable car up to the Aiguille du Midi was being discussed at the beginning of the century. But when an Italian engineer, Dino Lora Totino, Count of Cervinia, suggested doing it with only two spans of cable – one of which would be the longest unbroken cable in the world – no one believed him. But that is what finally happened.

A steel cable 1700 metres (5,580 feet) long was actually carried up the mountain by guides from Chamonix and Aosta. Twenty mountaineers took part in the two-day struggle. The weather did not help. Towards the end, there were arctic conditions, gales and snowstorms. But somehow – in spite of two fatal accidents – they succeeded. The world's (then) highest cable car opened in 1955. Three years later the Aiguille du Midi was in turn linked with Courmayeur (Italy) after further super-human construction work produced the Vallée Blanche Cable Car which linked with the new Col du Geant Cable Car on the Italian side.

But in spite of its dramatic history and scenery, the Aiguille du Midi/Vallée Blanche combination by no means provides all the excitement. There is a classic run in the original Chamonix ski area of Brévent. Descending through 1500 vertical metres (4,920 feet), it drops severely via Planpraz down an exposed wall, through a narrow gulley and then on down a further extremely long stretch of mogul fields.

Peace in the Chamonix Valley. In spite of its machismo image, it's not all grunt-and-groan skiing.

The Fiégère area, towards Argentière also has some challenging skiing, including some good off-piste. And the run down from the top of L'Index to the valley floor below has some wonderful views of the Aiguille du Midi and Mont Blanc.

For those with a real sense of adventure, it is even possible to ski down Mont Blanc itself. (It was first climbed in 1786 by Paccard and Balmat.) There are at least three routes, one of which is suitable for even moderately expert skiers. A guide is absolutely essential. But since helicopter skiing around Mont Blanc has now been banned on all sides – France, Italy and Switzerland – the only way up now is to walk.

Even this is no guarantee that you will actually be able to ski Mont Blanc. The weather is traditionally unpredictable in the area and snow storms and strong winds can blow up when they are least expected. I once spent an entire week in Chamonix waiting in vain for the right weather conditions for an attempt by helicopter from the Italian side, and I was bitterly disappointed and frustrated not to be able to attempt a descent.

It was during a 'rehearsal' that I experienced one of skiing's worst nightmares. High on an Italian glacier, Bionnassay, having just been dropped off by helicopter, I suddenly fell through the snow and found myself dropping like a boulder into a crevasse. One moment I was skiing in deep powder under a dazzlingly blue sky in bright sunshine – the next I was falling into a dark, icy chasm.

Fortunately my fall was broken by a snow bridge. But for some time no one knew where I was until I managed to launch one of my skis through the hole I had made in the snow six metres (twenty feet) above me. Until then my shouts for help and theirs trying to locate me had gone unheard. Snow muffles sound ruthlessly.

I was pulled out by one of our excellent guides, Jean-Paul Ollagnier. (The other guide was Jean Marc Boivin, one of the very small handful of men who has skied down the Matterhorn and survived. Recently he has also skied the equally terrifying Chamonix peak of Aiguille du Dru and parapented from the top of Everest.) Ollagnier threw down several ropes for me to loop around my legs and arms. In spite of the fact that he had parts of his fingers missing after being caught with the ski-extreme expert, Sylvain Saudan, in a terrible avalanche in the Himalayas, he managed to drag me out bodily, splendidly assisted by Eddie Laxton, a tough ex-rugby player who took the considerable strain.

That evening Saudan expressed amazement that just two men had managed to rescue me. 'A man like that' he said, looking at my fifteen-stone frame, 'would normally need about five people to get him out.' I was very fortunate. But I have not learnt my lesson. I *still* cannot wait to ski Mont Blanc. Another day, perhaps. As they told me in Chamonix, it has to be when the mountain is 'ready'. Otherwise I might end up inside another of her countless crevasses.

The first fatal accident on Mont Blanc happened in 1820, when five guides fell into a crevasse on the Grand Plateau. An English geologist, James Forbes, predicted that three bodies which were not found at the time would emerge between thirty-five and forty years later. After forty-one years the huge Bossons Glacier surrendered their bodies. For them, certainly, there was no escape.

After my most recent trip to Chamonix in 1989, I found it more enthralling than ever. Like many others, I suspect I have developed a love-hate relationship with the place. But I suspect that love will always win – and lure me back again and again.

SKI FACTS

RESORT HEIGHT	1000 m
RANGE	1050 – 3842 m
BLACK RUNS	5
RED RUNS	19
BLUE RUNS	13
GREEN RUNS	6
TOTAL	43
PISTES	250 km
LIFTS	34

COURCHEVEL

Très snob. Très chic. Beacoup de Gallic shrug. And rather full of its own importance, like some of the people who ski there. However, it would be impossible – not to mention churlish – to leave Courchevel out of any book about world-class resorts because the skiing is undeniably excellent and the resort is a classic.

Courchevel is fur coat and gold watch country, with pampered *Parisienne* poodles (animal and human variety) and, last time I was there, some sixteen boutiques, about eight up-market hairdressers, half a dozen or so jewellers, at least seven nightclubs, more than a hundred hotels and restaurants and of course beautifully manicured pistes. As in St Moritz, its Swiss counterpart, the rich can fly in direct.

Not only does Courchevel have some of the best skiing in the French Alps, it is also part of one of the most fabulous skiing areas in the world – the famous Trois Vallées (*Le Plus Grand Domaine Skiable du Monde* – give or take the other claimant to the same title, the Portes du Soleil – see Avoriaz.)

This means that three other great skiing areas are within easy reach. Méribel-Mottaret, just a hop and a skip over La Saulire and, somewhat further afield, the huge, bleak but excellent ski areas of Val Thorens and Les Menuires. You must ensure that you set out in good time for the return journey. If you miss the connecting lift, the taxi fare will make a nasty dent in your holiday funds.

It is difficult to imagine a greater contrast than that between Courchevel, with its delicious scenery, runs beautifully groomed like a French sex-kitten's finger nails, excitingly skiable couloirs and chicest of Parisian atmospheres, and Val Thorens at the other end of the Trois Vallées, with its vast, sometimes even scarey lunar landscapes where the skiing is every bit as challenging as that at Courchevel and yet feels, looks and *is* almost totally different.

Altogether the Trois Vallées cover around two hundred lifts which serve some 500 kilometres (310 miles) of pisted runs plus huge areas of off-piste

Skiing for pampered Parisiennes.

Opposite
Courchevel – fabulous skiing amid magnificent scenery.

skiing. Courchevel, a classic 'second generation' ski resort which opened in 1947, is a paradise for beginners and timid intermediates and yet has enough tough and exhilarating skiing to keep the advanced skiers happy too. And of course they can venture further afield to the other ski resorts to achieve an even greater variety of skiing. The only problem is that the really testing alternatives are mainly at the other end of the Trois Vallées in Val Thorens.

Probably the best compromise is to stay in neither, but plump for accommodation in Méribel-Mottaret. Not only is it cheaper than Courchevel and far less bleak than Val Thorens, but it is also a perfect springboard for either.

Depending on the weather conditions, how good, bad or late a night you have had, and your mood in general, you can either hop over to the comforting resort of Courchevel and pamper yourself on and off the slopes, or set out with grim determination like a Himalayan climber (oxygen not compulsory) for the tough but awe-inspiring heights of Val Thorens (Europe's highest resort) or Les Menuires.

Not, as I have said, that Courchevel lacks its own tough skiing. It has a lot of excellent couloir skiing above the Combe de Saulire for a start, three of which (Petit, Grand and Emile Allais) are quite skiable in good conditions by brave and sound advanced-intermediates. (Guide strongly recommended.) Another, directly under the huge radio mast, is much more fearsome and narrow, and you should not go near it without a guide. In fact you probably should not go near it even *with* a guide.

The couloirs are reached in Courchevel's huge new cable car which runs up to Saulire (2708 metres; 8,884 feet) every four minutes (except when it breaks down), carries up to 160 people and claims (like a few others) to be the largest in the world.

Another splendid descent for off-piste buffs is the Col du Fruit (technically in the Meribel Valley but reached from Courchevel). The approach to this huge snowfield is more unsettling than the descent itself. You have to climb and traverse a

Courchevel – the smart end of the Trois Vallées complex.

long, sometimes slightly severe ridge which at one stage can necessitate taking your skis off and carrying them. With a sheerish drop on both sides, it is better not to look down – but if you don't, you miss some wonderful scenery.

The panaroma is stunning, and there in the distance you can pick out quite clearly the cable car at the top of the Cime de Caron, the pride of Val Thorens, and the Aiguille de Peclet at 3562 metres (11,686 feet) where the highest skiing in the Trois Vallées takes place.

The actual col is a seemingly endless, but not terrifyingly steep snowfield. The problem is that there is no certain way to gauge the snow conditions before you arrive. If conditions are not good you are more or less stuck – sometimes almost literally – with the descent anyway. Sometimes, of course, on such a long run, conditions can change half-way down.

The last time I skied it, all seemed well at the top, and we were confident enough to 'let go' and commit ourselves to a series of sweeping linked turns. Half way down we hit breakable crust. It became a nightmare for one of our party who was less experienced than the rest of us in deep snow – or deep crust, I should say.

The descent eventually took him two and a half hours and by the time he reached the bottom he was utterly exhausted. However, his unfortunate experience should not put keen skiers off what can be a memorable run for joyful reasons rather than unhappy ones. Just try to make a careful guess – your guide's job of course – about whether the col is going to be agony or ecstasy.

If, however, like my friend, you prefer in future to stick to the piste, Courchevel offers a huge amount of skiing spread widely across the mountains with enormous variety. There are almost endless runs for beginners and intermediates. In her book *The World's Greatest Ski Holidays*, Elisabeth Hussey writes 'Some of the wide boulevards are so gentle that the most geriatric of skiers can slide slowly down, enjoying the sunshine and the mountain views without fear of falling.'

For those who want something a little more exciting but not quite in the couloir class, there is quite a selection of powerful runs such as the celebrated Jean Blanc with a 914-metre (3,000-foot) vertical drop. Other challenging runs worthy of note include Chanrossa (famous for its moguls) Jockeys, 'M' and Les Suisses.

There are actually three Courchevels (not counting the original village at 1300 metres; 4,265 feet): Courchevel 1550, 1650 and 1850 where the bulk of the skiing takes place. In a week of skiing without so much as crossing into Méribel, even an industrious intermediate could never ski the resort out.

Courchevel, some seventy-two miles from Geneva, is quite high – 1844 metres (6,050 feet) but its next-door-but-one neighbour Val Thorens is the highest resort in Europe at 2300 metres (7,544 feet), as distinct from Davos, Switzerland which claims to be the highest *town*. Courchevel likes gadgets and the latest technology. Apart from its famous Saulire cable car (opened December 1984) the resort has twenty-one piste-grooming machines and more than two hundred artificial-snow cannons. And there is plenty to do there if you do not ski, as I discovered when I sustained one of my few injuries.

Fat cat resort or not, it is all rather delectable.

SKI FACTS

RESORT HEIGHT	1550 m; 1650 m; 1850 m
RANGE	1300 – 2708 m
BLACK RUNS	9
RED RUNS	32
BLUE RUNS	22
GREEN RUNS	23
TOTAL	86
LIFTS	61

FLAINE

From Flaine you can ski the whole Grand Massif.

Flaine, in the heart of Le Grand Massif, is a homely, unpretentious, user-friendly and enjoyable resort which is extremely popular with the British and considered by some to be a little less ghastly in design than some purpose-built French resorts. Others, however, do find it ugly – so in the end it is all somewhat subjective.

In a sense it is Flaine's extraordinary ordinariness which makes it special. There is almost nothing wrong with it, which sounds rather bland and negative, but in fact this is one of its strengths.

The skiing is really rather good, can be excellent, there is plenty of it (250 kilometres (155 miles) of marked pistes served by more than sixty lifts – in the region) and the transfer time from Geneva is mercifully quick (about two hours). Its other major strength is its superb off-piste skiing. Flaine, one of

the original purpose-built resorts, would probably not quite qualify as a top world resort if its off-piste opportunities were not taken into consideration.

Having had the supreme good fortune to find myself invited to ski there with a party of demented French Canadians, I revelled in some of the best powder-skiing I have ever experienced in my life. All these years later – though I have revisited it very recently to make sure I was not dreaming – I can still feel a warm glow thinking about that week, which is why I cannot leave it out of this book.

Our guide resembled the skinny young man who used to get sand kicked in his face in the Charles Atlas advertisements. He also sported National Health-style spectacles. But he skied like a warrior.

The Canadians, who had won their trip here in a competition, were brilliant skiers who seemed determined to test the laws of gravity, survival and sanity in their attempts to drown themselves in a snowy Nirvana.

One of the great joys of skiing in deep, steep powder is that you can get away with almost anything . . . leaping off cliffs, skiing near-vertical drops, disappearing in a flurry of seemingly bottomless, tingling, talcum-like snow, and occasionally coming up for crisp air like a beached whale.

The Canadians urged, egged and even tormented each other on, sometimes even deliberately encouraging and engineering each other's downfall. They would guide one of the party into a trap, only to burst out with uncontrollable laughter when the victim ended up doing a 'head-plant' (involuntarily diving head first into the snow) in the middle of nowhere. Thanks to these wild and amusing Canadians, it was here in Flaine that I discovered that with the right snow and the right company in the right resort, skiing can take on a breathtaking and surreal quality which is as close to sporting ecstasy as I can imagine.

But yet again – especially in Flaine, where the off-piste terrain, with the occasional cliff and pothole is more dangerous than some – I must risk repeating myself by stressing the importance of only skiing off-piste with an instructor or guide.

On-piste, Flaine's skiing has been 'pepped up' fairly recently (1985) with the introduction of the twenty-three-person gondola/cable car hybrid which can speed three thousand skiers an hour up to Grandes Platières – the type which is gradually being installed in more and more French resorts.

Links with other villages – Samoëns, Morillon and Les Carroz are available – have also put a lot of extra 'flesh' on the resort's ski area. Some of these runs, particularly down to Morillon, are easy, relaxed and scenic runs through the woods, which makes a refreshing change from much of the skiing in Flaine itself, which tends to be mainly above the tree-line. Others, especially from the top towards Samoëns, are quite tough, both on- and off-piste.

The resort itself is divided into two sections – Flaine Forêt and the traffic-free area of Flaine Forum, which are linked by a free space-age shuttle, The Red Devil, which operates day and night. Flaine, the highest of the Grand Massif resorts, is built at 1600 metres (5,250 feet) and the skiing reaches 2500 metres (8,200 feet). In the Grand Massif area there are some thirty-three blue runs, forty-five red and fourteen black.

They have had the quaint notion of naming many of their runs after a devilish theme – hell! Thus you can ski such diabolical runs as Lucifer, Mephisto, Diable and Belzebuth. But even these descents can be heavenly in good snow conditions.

The Aujon area often has good off-piste skiing (as well as wide open pistes for those who do not want to stray in the footsteps of mad Canadians) and there is also some excellent 'out-of-bounds' skiing in the Vernant direction. Gers, always unpisted and not infrequently closed, also provides some wonderful off-piste, and so does the Grands Vans side of Flaine. The Tête de Véret has a couple of quite testing blacks which are even more fun when they are left unpisted.

Some people turn their noses up at Flaine, but there is a lot of good skiing there and it truly is a wonderful resort for encouraging intermediate skiers to become really proficient.

It also happens to be a friendly and enjoyable ski resort, no matter what the purists say.

SKI FACTS

RESORT HEIGHT	1600 m
RANGE	1600 – 2500 m
BLACK RUNS	6
RED RUNS	18
BLUE RUNS	10
GREEN RUNS	3
TOTAL	37
LIFTS	30

flaine
1600/2500 M
haute-savoie
france

LA GRAVE

La Grâve is breathtaking, wild and unique. It is not really a skiing resort at all as such, but an old climbing village which skiers have somehow managed to infiltrate.

My first glimpse of La Grâve was during my return from a visit to Montgenevre via the spectacularly beautiful Col de Lautaret. If you stop in the picturesque village, with its narrow streets and twelfth-century Romanesque church, and crane your neck almost vertically, an astonishing sight greets your eyes. There, towering above you is a huge, wild and rocky mountain range. Almost incredibly, looking the size of the tiniest of toy models, a microscopic collection of bubble lifts can be spotted climbing like skylarks into the heavens. Can these really be ski-lifts with mere mortals inside them? It looks impossibly steep and there seems to be an ocean of sky and space between these tiny pin-prick gondolas and the ground below.

You are not, however, imagining things. And when you climb aboard one of these Téléphérique de la Meije bubble cars, it transports you across the rushing waters of the Romanche up to the Col des Ruillans 3200 metres (10,500 feet) into an extraordinary, chillingly beautiful glacial paradise which falls steeply away from the mighty Meije almost 4000 metres (13,123 feet) on the other side of Les Deux Alpes.

Even Edward Whymper, who conquered the Matterhorn, found La Meije too powerful for him, and when it was finally climbed in 1887 it was the last of the major Alpine peaks to be climbed.

La Grave: frightening, remote and stunningly beautiful.

Awesome in winter, idyllic in summer – a place of extremes, not for the faint hearted.

The slopes of La Grave are gruelling and totally ungroomed. There are no pistes and no piste grooming machines. You feel privileged to share a great mountain climbing area with the climbers themselves. Everywhere you look the scenery is larger than life. Huge glaciers and moraine fields stare down at you as you ski, feeling like an Alpine Tom Thumb, down the vast snowfields at the base of these jagged peaks. Seracs add an almost demented jaggedness to the scene. Without your guide you would not only be unsafe – you would also feel very much alone in a powerful, beautiful but almost alien world.

On your right, the route takes you through powder and hardpacked snow until your knees ache. You return in the bubbles, strung together like a row of beads, bobbing impossibly high above the desolate landscape, to try another route, this time to the left. Now it is row upon row of deep moguls that you must contend with. The legs ache even more. The scenery remains truly spectacular.

My instructor, Regis, glances behind to see how I am faring. There are just the two of us, and the altitude, endless bumps and sometimes severe snow conditions are tiring. But what a feeling when we are down! The sense of achievement is exquisite. The skiing has been relentless rather than severe. The scenery quite overpowering. And to share all this with a single mountain guide was an experience never to be forgotten.

Behind us, a skiing domaine that seems utterly awe inspiring. Should the gods ever seek a location for *Götterdämmerung*, La Grâve would surely be a prime candidate. Which makes it all the more startling that it should be within the grasp of mere mortals.

LA PLAGNE

Like a desert of snow, La Grande Plagne goes on for ever. If ever a resort epitomized a third-generation purpose-built ski area, it would be difficult to find one more appropriate. It is also a good example of traditional villages being linked with a purpose-built ski area. This enables skiers, if they so desire, at least to spend their night hours in a traditional atmosphere rather than remain in a 'space-age' ski metropolis when they have done with its slopes for the day.

There are in fact a number of 'villages' which make up the resort (ten if you include the three genuinely traditional villages down in the valley: Champagny, Montchavin and Montalbert) varying in style from the would-be rustic design of Belle Plagne to the brave-and-startling-new-world concept of the resort's flagship, Aime la Plagne. This does actually look like a ship, especially at night when, illuminated, it could easily be taken for a huge ocean-going liner that has beached itself high and dry on a vast rock outcrop. The five high-mountain villages are linked all day until 1.00 am by either cable car 'telebus' or a shuttle.

The original complex of La Plagne (1800 metres; 5,905 feet) claims to be the longest-established purpose-built ski resort in France. Building started

of man-made environment that settlers who may one day colonize the moon and planets could experience.

There must have been a little soul searching when they started work on this trend-setting complex – a model for so many future developments – about how much to pander to those who were used to the traditional après-ski ambiance of conventional first- and second-generation resorts.

The après-ski in some purpose-built resorts that followed La Plagne is conspicious by its silence, although not everyone finds that such a bad thing. Indeed hardy skiers of the more conservative breed are used to going to France for good skiing and peaceful nights.

But La Plagne has made an effort to introduce artificially as much night life as possible. Thus there are several discothèques, at least two piano bars, film shows and festivals, crêperies and restaurants of all descriptions. Again, the metaphor of a space station being equipped for the recreational needs of space colonists is not inappropriate.

The actual skiing area, from 1250 metres to 3250 metres (4,000 feet – 10,630 feet), with almost 100 lifts and at least 200 kilometres (125 miles) of groomed piste (predominantly north-facing) is immense, and although sometimes unexciting and predictable, it is difficult to imagine any skier of any ability being dissatisfied. There are more than 100 marked runs and most of them are reds; seven are black and the rest blue. The remaining seven are classified as difficult.

One of the pleasant aspects of a resort comprising a cluster of villages is that it is fun to ski from one to

there as long ago as 1961. The site is a dramatic one: it was here in 1944 that there was a big arms drop to the Maquis.

The residential area, especially in Aime, is almost totally self contained under one roof, so that once you have finished skiing for the day, every requirement from cinema to restaurant, disco, slot-machines and bed can be reached without venturing out again into the arctic and barren waste outside.

Living and relaxing in such a mountain-metropolis can be exciting but strangely unsettling. One can easily imagine similarities to living in the kind

La Plagne may not win prizes for its architecture but the extent of the skiing is impressive.

the other – a concept denied to lesser skiers in some single-village resorts.

La Plagne, a mere ninety miles from Geneva, is one of the hosts for the forthcoming Winter Olympics in 1992.

It is something of an oasis on the Trans-Tarentaise route which takes skiers on a week-long trek across the Tarentaise mountains, usually from Tignes to Les Menuires. (The ordinary lift pass allows you time at Tignes, Val d'Isère and Les Arcs.)

I remember how La Plagne loomed into sight after hours of skiing in the snowy wilderness *en route* from Les Arcs. Suddenly, there it was, stretched out in front of us – a very welcome sight.

The resort is sometimes criticized for its bland skiing. I would disagree. The runs may not be of the kamikaze version, but they are long and usually

La Plagne offers endless acres of easy skiing – and a few surprises!

nique quite happily without being over stretched.

Later you can graduate – with a guide – to Le Friolin, a breathtaking vertical 2000-metre (6,561-feet) off-piste descent fifteen kilometres (nine miles) long from the Bellecôte Glacier down to Peisey. There is also an excitingly steep 700-metre (2,296-foot) descent from Aime-La-Plagne to La Roche.

Big is not always beautiful, and purpose-built resorts are never so ... But just as not everyone would agree that Les Menuires is a 'smile', few would think of Aime as being terribly lovable. But La Plagne has got a great deal going for it. Skiing for everybody, and almost a different village for every taste too. A little like Vail, Colorado (although not quite in the same league) La Plagne really is a 'something-for-everybody' resort.

quite tricky enough to give most skiers something to get their teeth into. And, after all, it is often the skier as much as the run that can create the difficulty. Given an average descent, there are always ways of choosing the most difficult line in order to relieve any tedium.

Besides, La Plagne – especially in the Bellecôte area – has some delightful runs off-piste through the trees where one can practise one's powder tech-

SKI FACTS

RESORT HEIGHT	1900 m
RANGE	1250 – 3250 m
BLACK RUNS	7
RED RUNS	95
BLUE RUNS	13
TOTAL	115
PISTES	200 km
LIFTS	100
LONGEST RUN	15 km

la Plagne
toute la montagne en 10 stations

LES ARCS

The elegant and futuristic resort of Les Arcs, with its gloriously wide open spaces over-looking the Haute Tarentaise Valley is one of the most dynamic of the French resorts. There is a zing and a zeal about it that almost guarantees a lack of boredom, at least on the slopes. Its critics, however, say the après-ski is dull.

The resort, dreamt up by Robert Blanc who died tragically prematurely in an avalanche in 1979, is famous for pioneering the so-called 'Ski-Evolutif' method of learning to ski, which revolutionized the old Austro/Swiss concept that you should hold your hand aloft, and your skis should be as high. The concept is simple and effective. But there are logistic complications.

On the first day you start with very short skis (a metre long) which are easy to turn on but less stable than longer skis. You quickly move up to a slightly longer ski (135s) then 160s, and so on, gradually balancing the stability of a longer ski with the turning ability of a short one.

The theory is that when people start learning to ski, the most difficult stumbling block is trying to turn. The shorter the ski, however, the easier this manoeuvre becomes. Once the student has learned how to turn using short skis, he or she will gradually become confident enough to turn on the longer skis which will eventually be required to achieve stability at speed.

At this stage the novice should no longer be worrying about how to turn and therefore should no longer need to rely on the shortness of the skis to be able to do so. Each day longer skis are used until the near normal length of 180 centimetres is appropriate.

It certainly works. The problem lies in trying to persuade resorts to phase out many of their conventional skis and replace them with costly stocks of Evolutif skis. It is largely this snag that has prevented the idea from catching on in any really significant way.

If it's exotic, Les Arcs skis it!

So, having learnt to ski using one method or the other, what does Les Arcs have to offer? There are three sections: Arc Pierre Blanche 1600, Arc Chantel 1800 and the bowl area of Arc 2000.

Arc 1600, nestling in a woodland hollow, has just been linked with Bourg-St-Maurice by the new 'Arc en Ciel' funicular which takes a mere seven minutes. The area has some fairly steep skiing, much of it through pine and larch trees.

Arc 1800's runs are more open and easier, and even Arc 2000 has some easyish runs which can be enjoyed, along with the scenery, by very moderate skiers. But this area is also the location for the toughest and most challenging mountain in the Arcs' portfolio, the Aiguille Rouge – the location for what is claimed to be the longest black run in the world, 2500 metres (8,200 feet) down to Bourg-St-Maurice. It is also the home of Europe's best known 'kilometre lancée' (flying kilometre) course. Mere holiday-makers and humble ski writers such as myself can actually indulge their quest for glory here.

The professionals, clad in aerodynamic, thin plastic suits, Darth Vader visors and clamped into gigantic 237-centimetre skis surge down a steep run-in above the flying kilometre course which starts with a ninety per cent gradient. When they reach the top of the actual measured kilometre they are already travelling at high speed. They can reach speeds of up to 134 mph as they hit the fastest stretch. However, 'punters' can – and indeed really ought to – ignore this top section and start the run from the beginning of the actual kilometre itself.

Even having taken this obvious precaution, one can achieve a somewhat frightening speed (frightening, at least, for the likes of you and me). I clocked sixty miles per hour and found this quite sufficient excitement for a forty-plus-year-old!

One or two tips worth passing on: do not ski too close behind the person in front of you. The spray from his skis may temporarily blind you, and a collision at even this speed is not a good idea. Do not try to turn or stop or indeed do anything except

Not as unsightly as some purpose-built accommodation, but the French do tend to cram more people into apartments than the Swiss.

go straight, otherwise you will almost certainly fall over and break something. The hill at the bottom will provide all the breaking power you need.

From the Aiguille Rouge, with its recently installed cable car, you can also attempt one of the longest descents in the world – the seventeen-kilometre run down a huge 2296-metre (7,533-foot) vertical drop to Villaroger.

Of the 150 kilometres (93 miles) of marked runs, the region has ten green runs, thirty runs are blue, thirty-seven are red and there are twenty black runs. The ski area includes the four valleys of Villaroger, Arc 2000, Bourg-St-Maurice and Peisey-Nancroix.

Should you desire further variety, you may visit the neighbouring resort of La Plagne on the same lift pass, and you can enjoy a one-day excursion to Val d'Isère/Tignes. The pass now also covers the excellent French/Italian resort of La Rosière-La Thuile. There is also some superb and extremely testing off-piste skiing, particularly from the Grand Col.

Les Arcs, with 15,000 hectares (37,000 acres) of skiing from 1600 metres (5,250 feet) up to 3226 metres (9,800 feet), seventy-six lifts and ninety-five trails has always been a very go-ahead resort with all kinds of skiing innovations. It is, they will tell you, 'more than just a resort: it is an attitude of mind!' Much of the current impetus towards such skiing spin-offs as mono-skiing, snowboarding, and skiing with parachutes either originated or was encouraged here in a way which was originally frowned upon by the more traditional Swiss and Austrians. This has crystalized into a concept entitled 'La Glisse' (gliding on skis). The 'Apocolypse Snow' ski school teaches mono-skiing, ski surf, ski extreme, helicopter skiing and powder and couloir skiing.

I vividly remember trying something called 'Ski Bird' in Les Arcs. This involved attaching sturdy plastic 'wings' or shields to your arms. Suddenly you seemed able to ski straight down even a difficult black, using the wings not to fly but to slow down your velocity. They had the dramatic, lunar-like effect of reducing your weight so that you skimmed bumps and cornices with the greatest of ease, not to mention speed. You steered by lowering the appropriate arm.

It was an exhilarating experience, but you had to be careful when you took your wings off. While they were on, you had experienced an almost omnipotent feeling that you could ski down anything. Without their protection, however, you suddenly became a mere mortal again. Black runs suddenly had their normal capacity to terrify restored to them. The magic carpet had once again become a dull and lifeless rug.

Les Arcs, as befits front runners in skiing concepts, has been quick to follow the Americans love of floodlit skiing. You can now ski at night on the Piste du Lac des Combes (Arc 2000) the Piste du Charvet (Arc 1800) and the Pistes des Combettes at Arc 1600.

Although only five hours from Paris by the new fast train link (TGV), getting to Les Arcs by other means can be extremely tiresome, as it can be to nearby Val d'Isère and Tignes. The coach ride from Geneva is usually at least four hours because the access road from Albertville is clogged up at weekends with the most awful traffic jams. However, because Albertville is hosting the Winter Olympics in 1992, a new four-lane road is due to open in 1991.

But for Les Arcs, I would sit patiently on a coach for days. In fact I seem to remember that I did.

SKI FACTS

RESORT HEIGHT	1800 m
RANGE	1610 – 3226 m
BLACK RUNS	15
RED RUNS	22
BLUE RUNS	8
TOTAL	45
PISTES	150 km
LIFTS	73
LONGEST RUN	17 km

LES DEUX ALPES

When I first glimpsed Les Deux Alpes, perched high on the edge of a cliff with its lights twinkling in the dusk, it was like a scene from *Close Encounters*. From the Col de Lautaret pass, it seemed as though an entire space city was hovering in the heavens above me. In broad daylight the following day, the reality was nowhere near so romantic. But the skiing is exciting.

Like Alpe d'Huez, its neighbour just across the Romanche Valley, the resort of Les Deux Alpes is a big, impressive, top-flight ski area with wonderful scenery, good snow and slopes which cannot fail to please skiers of every standard. The British love it almost as much as the French (who tend to swarm into it in force at weekends) and it features in almost every major British tour operator's brochure. (Odd that its neighbour Alpe d'Huez, which is just as good if not better, does not.)

Formerly two separate farming communities, Mont de Lans and Alpe de Venosc, the area stretches out at 1650 metres (5,143 feet) along its high, often sunny shelf, or saddle. It is surrounded by the steep slopes of the Massif des Ecrins in the upper Dauphine, and dominated by the magnificent peak of La Meije (3983 metres; 13,068 feet).

Although the resort, developed in the fifties, falls into the purpose-built category, it cannot be bracketed with the space-age architecture which some skiers find so ugly in resorts such as La Plagne, Flaine and Avoriaz. However, the resort is hardly what one could call pretty.

Les Deux Alpes: perched high on the edge of a cliff.

Opposite
View from a mogul.

There are two main ski areas: Pied Moutet, which tends to attract beginners, on the western side, and the eastern side where most of the 'real' skiing is. The focal uphill transport here is the state-of-the-art Jandri Express – something of a cross between a gondola and a cable car which speeds around 1,800 passengers an hour up to the glacier. The journey takes twenty minutes.

Some of the skiing is very high – up to 3568 metres (11,660 feet), with wonderful views of Mont Blanc. There is a link with the unique mountain resort of La Grave (see page 54) where the skiing is totally unpisted and set in the most spectacular and awe-inspiring glacial scenery. This excursion should neither be missed by the adventurous skier nor undertaken without a guide.

The lower slopes of Les Deux Alpes are wide but often steep, though oddly enough the higher you go, the easier many of the runs tend to be. Up on the glacier of Mont de Lans, a noted summer skiing area (though it can become pretty cold even in the sunshine) the skiing is much gentler, and even novices can manage some of the runs. This is a bonus for them. In most resorts trainee skiers rarely experience the thrill of 'going to the top'

The British love the place almost as much as the French.

because so often the nursery slopes are the lowest in the resort. Squaw Valley, California has a similar quality.

Les Deux Alpes has one of the highest vertical drops in the Alps, with a near 2000-metre (6,560-foot) difference between the village and the highest lift. This enables skiers to accomplish a magnificent nine-mile run. The seventy-five runs comprise more than 170 kilometres (105 miles) of marked piste served by more than sixty lifts.

Les Deux Alpes' new pride and joy, the Dome Express, is now the second highest funicular in Europe. It was opened during the winter of 1989/90. Engineers had to carve a 1.6-kilometre tunnel through the Dome de Puy Salie to extend the already impressive Jandri Express. The tourist office is extremely excited about its new toy which it believes will make their resort the best in Europe. They are of course, a little biased. But it is one of less than a handful of funiculars in the world to be built under a glacier, and follows the construction of Val d'Isère's popular Funival.

If in spite of all this excitement and huge skiing potential, you still feel like a change, your lift pass covers excursions to Alpe d'Huez, Puy St Vincent, Serre Chevalier, Montgenèvre and Sestriere, Italy.

There is almost no limit to the challenging runs on offer to keen skiers. Le Diable and Le Grand Couloir are particularly worth mentioning. And there is a particularly good, long run off-piste to the village of Venosc.

The off-piste in general is plentiful and among the best in Europe, particularly around Les Gourses. Apart from Le Grand Couloir, there are a number of other daunting couloirs – one of which came close to paralyzing me with something remarkably similar to fear – and at least ten stimulating black runs such as the Serre Palace mogul run.

Among the more usual 'fitness' features provided to tone up aching limbs after a day of hectic skiing in this resort is the unusual innovation of 'sensory-depravation', better known as 'tanking.' For fifty minutes you are immersed in a huge tank with water at body temperature, and there is neither sight nor sound apart from your own heart beat. It sounds as though this might drive you slowly insane, but converts swear to its therapeutic qualities, and claim it is as good as a night's sleep.

In theory – and in fact quite easily in practice – you could ski Alpe d'Huez in the morning, take a four-minute helicopter ride to Les Deux Alpes, pop over the top to La Grâve, ski that and then ski Les Deux Alpes for the rest of the afternoon. You would have skied three of the finest resorts in Europe in one day. Something similar, of course, is done every day by hundreds of skiers in Les Trois Vallées. But it would still be a rapturous experience.

I suppose sooner or later most of the French Alps will be joined up like a 'Dotto' game into one big ski resort. Let us hope it is later.

SKI FACTS

RESORT HEIGHT	1650 m
RANGE	1282 – 3560 m
BLACK RUNS	10
RED RUNS	16
BLUE RUNS	30
GREEN RUNS	19
TOTAL	75
PISTES	170 km
LIFTS	59
LONGEST RUN	14.4 km

TIGNES/ VAL D'ISERE

Val d'Isère. Just saying those words sends a tingle down many a spine, including mine. Just 'Val' would do. It is the only ski resort of many in France prefixed with Val that is instantly recognizable to any self-respecting skier as being the one and only Val d'Isère.

As I write this, I have just returned from my latest pilgrimage to this skiing mecca. As ever, the skiing was superb. Although nothing could quite match the week I spent there in 1984.

During that most memorable of occasions – it happened to coincide with my fortieth birthday – my skiing, and that of my three close skiing friends, was transformed almost overnight. It could do that for anyone willing to surrender to its fabulous skiing opportunities. It is that kind of place.

That week was a unique cocktail of perfect snow, cloudless blue skies, and the kind of cameraderie that can happen when friends, (three men and a girl, in this case) experience a breathtaking, exhilarating skiing adventure, going through fear, fitness and even pain barriers together. It was a wonderful experience made possible by our young instructor, Daniel Hansjacob. Although he looked like a fresh-faced boy just out of *lycée*, he had an uncanny ability to motivate all of us and stretch us to our limits without ever risking our necks.

Sir Arnold Lunn, in his book *The Mountains of Youth* (1925), summed up the joys of skiing with three friends, and I could not put it better. He was describing a glacier run in the Bernese Oberland, but it could apply anywhere.

> For many months the four of us had skied together, and sometimes one and sometimes another had skied well. But this was one of those days when the four of us were skiing on the top of our form.
>
> There is a subtle joy in doing something delightful not as an individual, but as a member of a team, a pleasure that is nowhere greater than in skiing, especially when you know your friend's skiing as thoroughly as

Skiing taken to its outer limits!

you know his jokes, his best swing as well as you know your own virtues, and his weak turns as completely as he knows your vices.

Solos have their charm, but there is a skiing joy known only to a quartet of friends, all of whom are moving well together, placing their swings at the right point, and neither over-running the leader nor impeding those that follow.

That was 1925. But now it was 1984 and Daniel was about to lure our quartet down the impossible – our first couloir. 'I thought for a moment that you were expecting us to ski down there,' I remember chuckling at him as we paused to peer over the edge of a particularly steep, fearsome-looking gulley, the Couloir de Chevreuil (Roe-Buck Gulley). He was. We suddenly stopped any semblance of chuckling.

'Do not be afraid' were his immortal words as one by one we crept over the edge of the abyss. He was waiting for us half-way down, as if to catch us if we fell. We knew he *could* have caught us because we had seen him catch someone almost twice as big as himself on an admittedly rather less steep slope that morning. And so began our initiation ritual. By the time it ended we were different skiers and even different people.

From time to time, the neighbouring resorts of Val and Tignes become cross with one another and sulk, which leads to a temporary 'skism' (excuse the pun) in the ski area and the introduction of two separate lift passes. The last hostilities, however, ended in 1982, when the two resorts kissed each other better with the following announcement: 'Big News: no more are Val d'Isère and Tignes the legendary enemis (sic) they once were. Better still, they are as one now, and their slogan for winter 1983–1984 will be "Killy's Space"' (After their great hero, Jean-Claude, although he was not actually born there.) And L'Espace Killy it has remained ever since.

Many believe that Val and Tignes (I've always wanted to re-christen them jointly as 'Valentine') comprise the greatest skiing area in Europe if not the world. Call it what you will: Val, Val and Tignes, or L'Espace Killy, Val d'Isère, like Aspen or Jackson Hole, is 'kind'a it' as far as European skiing is concerned.

It plays a vital role in the ski-racing circuit and indeed the first event in the World Cup calendar – *Le Criterium de la Première Neige* – is held here each December. Humbler but no less energetic fare comes later: Paris taxi drivers and then Marseilles police make their way here for their own downhill races.

A specialist alternative ski school, Top Ski, run by two ex-racers, Patrick and Jean Zimmer, even 'hire' the top half of the World Cup downhill course and hold a semi-serious downhill (with helmets and skis measuring anything from 213cm to 225cm) for all-comers, including serious racing types wearing plastic stretch racing suits, the odd ski instructor and even ageing *Financial Times* ski correspondents!

All the superlatives apply to Val. Within a ten-kilometre (six-mile) area, there are thirty-five peaks between 2987 metres (9,800 feet) and 3658 metres (12,000 feet). It has been said that Val d'Isère's red runs are other resorts' blacks.

The villages of Val d'Isère and Tignes may lack many things (especially charm), although Tignes is so modern that it actually makes Val, with its old quarter, attractive church and stone chalets look quite pretty by comparison. But on the slopes themselves, the riches are indeed embarrassingly good.

Off-piste skiers could spend weeks gorging themselves in the almost limitless 'back country', with spectacular runs like Le Tour du Charvet, Le Grand Vallon and the Col Pers. And they could treat themselves, if they so wished, to a different couloir every day, almost without ever skiing or even *seeing* a piste.

The Face de Bellevarde and the Epaule de Charvet are just two of the endless good on-piste runs I can recall, and the top of Toviere, now served by two telecabines, is the starting point for a number of good runs, including Paquerettes and Trolles. The Oeillet and Stade de Slalom runs down to Lac de Tignes are also recommended for good skiers.

Conventional skiers could and often do ski themselves dizzy on an almost endless network of pistes, and for once it really would undoubtedly be true – as so many resorts are fond of claiming – that you could spend weeks here without skiing the same run twice.

The Val/Tignes lift pass covers more than 110 lifts which serve 260 kilometres (160 miles) of marked pistes. There are 125 runs of which ten are black, ninety red and twenty-five blue.

La Daille, once just part of Val d'Isère's skiing area, has now become so big in its own right that it is treated more as a satellite of Val and considered to be almost a resort by itself. This is partly due to the recent installation of what is claimed to be the fastest funicular railway in the world, the Funival which takes around six and a half minutes (the blurb claims four) to return you and 271 other people to the top of the mountain. During my visit just before Christmas in 1988 it was still, however,

You can ski off-piste in Val d'Isère for as long as your legs can take the strain.

displaying teething problems. Because of the hydraulics, changing temperatures were causing it to break suddenly near the end of its ascent, sometimes hurling skiers against each other with considerable force. New electrically operated hydraulics are due to be installed in time for the 1989/90 season.

Val d'Isère was once a small hunting village owned by the Dukes of Savoie. The remnants of the old quarter linger on unobtrusively. The church dates back to 1533. Skiing started here as long ago as the 1930s, with the ski school opening in 1934.

Tignes, much the more recent, is purpose built. There was an old village of Tignes, but in 1952 it was 'moved' above the tree-line to a bowl at 2127 metres (6,980 feet) and renamed Lac de Tignes to make way for a large dam and the accompanying Lake Chevril, which now occupies the village's former location.

Modern Tignes (2100 metres; 6,890 feet) is split into a number of areas: Tignes itself, Lac de Tignes, Lavachet, Tignes les Boisses, Les Brévières and Val Claret from where you reach the famous Grande Motte glacier, the highest point in this vast ski area. The skiing here reaches 3475 metres (11,400 feet) and is one of Europe's classic summer-skiing areas. A new funicular is eventually likely to replace the ageing gondola system. Thanks to the glacier, Tignes is happy to boast that it offers skiing 365 days a year.

Although it is true that L'Espace Killy is a paradise for expert skiers, this is also true for intermediates. Even avoiding the area's celebrated black runs, many through the trees, there is an incredible wealth of comparatively easy skiing above the tree-line, and intermediate skiers who are fit enough can cover extraordinary distances without fully realizing it until they look at their lift maps in some amazement over dinner.

Tignes's infamous lunar landscape.

One of the most unusual runs in Val – Le Piste Perdu – follows the course of a narrow river, and is really a natural obstacle course between the rocks which delights children and tends to frustrate adults with its narrow switch-back course. You cannot really work up any speed but it is great fun trying to negotiate except when it is packed with youngsters all pausing at critical junctions on the route down.

The lift pass allows you a day's skiing in Les Arcs and La Plagne (and vice versa). It also includes a day in the splendid Italian (although it sounds and was at one stage – French) resort of La Thuile.

But quite why anyone should really want to go anywhere else except through idle curiosity, I cannot imagine. Why abandon the best champagne in Europe for fewer bubbles elsewhere?

However, beginners – although perfectly well catered for – would really be better off somewhere less extensive and expensive until they have picked up the rudiments of skiing. Quite honestly, to send a beginner to Val d'Isère and Tignes would be like sending a child with a bucket and spade to explore the Sahara.

Although the skiing is common to both Val d'Isere and Tignes, by no means all of the really testing runs are to be found in Val's territory. Val has its world-famous mogul field, know to Britons as the 'Solaise Bumps' but the moguls down Tovière in Tignes are claimed by devotees to be the most challenging in Europe.

Perhaps the most famous run in Tignes is the descent from the Aiguille Percée (a peak which has been eroded into the shape of the eye of a needle) down the Vallon de la Sache to Les Brévières. This breathtaking and steep run can be done on- or off-piste. Other challenging runs at Tignes include the Double M and the off-piste Tour de Pramecou.

SKI FACTS

RESORT HEIGHT	Tignes 2100 m
	Val d'Isère 1850 m
RANGE	1550 – 3440 m
BLACK RUNS	11
RED RUNS	90
BLUE RUNS	25
TOTAL	126
PISTES	260 km
LIFTS	110
LONGEST RUN	10 km

TIGNES

VAL THORENS/ Les Menuires

You either enjoy Val Thorens – perhaps appreciate is a better word than enjoy – or you do not. There is little room for faint praise. It is tough, dramatic, vast, relentless, desolate and – on a bad day – chilling, unfriendly, and sometimes even frightening.

Having said all these things, the skiing can be and usually is, superb. Val Thorens, one can safely say, is for serious skiers.

But whereas in Val d'Isère, for example, you do not have to experience a frisson of fear to seek out good skiing, at Val Thorens you sometimes do. It is not that the skiing itself is often frightening. It is the feel of the place. Its bleakness has prompted more than one person to describe it as 'like skiing on the moon.' Indeed it was only four years after man first set foot on the moon that Val Thorens's lunar landscape was opened for skiing (1973).

Val Thorens – correctly pronounced, surprisingly, Tor-Ens rather than Tor-On – has a soulless remoteness which is much to do with the fact that at 2300 metres (7,546 feet) it is the highest resort in Europe. It has skiing as high as 3430 metres (11,250 feet) and five glaciers in its terrain.

Courchevel, the sophisticated and people-pampering resort twenty-five miles of skiing away at the other end of the Trois Vallées system, might as well be on another planet. But the resort-next-door in the Trois Vallées system, Les Menuires, has a similar feel about it. Much of its skiing is linked with Val Thorens.

The five hundred or so vertical metres (1,640 feet) that separate the village of Val Thorens from the rather more sprawling Les Menuires can be critical. Last time I was there, in late December, Val Thorens had snow and Les Menuires did not. It was as simple as that. Skiing high above both resorts, we could see just how simple it was. The snow just stopped short of Les Menuires.

It was for this very scenario – and ironically during 1987, a year when winter made a par-

ticularly disastrous start – that the resort spent thirty-five million francs on what was claimed to be the world's first computer-operated snow-making machines.

Higher up in Les Menuires's skiing area, there was snow, particularly on La Masse (2278 metres; 7,473 feet), its best and toughest ski area.

Val Thorens, flanked on three sides by the Massif de la Vanoise, provides some of the most rugged skiing in the huge Trois Vallées five hundred-kilometre (310-mile) network, with over one hundred kilometres (62 miles) of marked pistes. The big skiing in the Val Thorens area centres on the Cime de Caron (3200 metres; 10,500 feet) served by one of the largest cable cars in the world.

The cable-car machinery at the peak – like some unwieldy relic from the industrial revolution – does not help to soften the contours of the skiing area, serving only to add to the arctic bleakness of the place. However, as long as the sun is shining, Val Thorens can be an exciting rather than a gloomy wilderness in which to find oneself. After all, in a sense, you *are* on top of the world.

There is good bump skiing off the Cascade run, and the skiing off the Boismint chair is also good. And there is a pleasant off-piste route all the way back to Meribel-Mottaret from Mont de la Chambre.

One of the best runs is from the recently opened Mont Vallon gondola (2952 metres; 9,685 feet). Both runs from the top are good – the one on the right is the tougher. There are excellent runs from the Aiguille de Peclet. In Val Thorens's own ski area there are 110 kilometres (68 miles) of marked runs served by more than thirty ski lifts. Of the thirty-six runs, seven are black, only three red, sixteen are blue and ten are green. Its neighbour, Les Menuires, has 100 kilometres (62

Beautiful but desolate – no place for the faint-hearted skier.

miles) of marked pistes and fifty-two runs, of which eight are black, thirty-one red, seven blue and six green.

There is some excellent skiing from Roc des Trois Marches and Mont de La Chambre which link with Meribel, but the classic runs are centred around La Masse and Pointe de la Masse (2804 metres; 9,200 feet), from where a clutch of steep and challenging black and red runs go thudding down towards the village.

Les Menuires is not an easy place to love. It has been described as one of the most ugly and dreary resorts in Europe. It even sounds distinctly un-attractive. But the French will have nothing said against it. They even refer to it, gallantly, as 'The Smile of the Three Valleys' – possibly, it has been suggested, because of the semicircular lay-out of the buildings.

One must not be unkind. Skiing on the moon or not, the runs are sturdy, challenging and gutsy, and as long as one can be secure in the expectation of a warm comfortable bed, a mug of hot chocolate and a warm, crackling fire at the end of the day, who cares about cuckoo clocks, yodelling and *gemutlichkeit*?

Actually, I do.

SKI FACTS

RESORT HEIGHT	2300 m
RANGE	1250 – 3400 m
BLACK RUNS	7
RED RUNS	3
BLUE RUNS	16
GREEN RUNS	10
TOTAL	36
PISTES	110 km
LIFTS	31
LONGEST RUN	8 km

CORTINA

It was perhaps a trifle unkind of the Ford Motor Company to name one of their more unfashionable cars after this most upmarket of ski resorts. Cortina – full name Cortina d'Ampezzo – is anything but unfashionable. Indeed it is Italy's answer – and a very real answer – to the likes of St Moritz, Lech and Aspen. It is therefore – unlike many Italian resorts – costly.

The Dolomites is a very special ski area with unique mountain scenery and Cortina is the undisputed skiing capital. It is quite a large town, with a traffic-free centre, which unlike some nearby locations, has never been part of the Austro-Hungarian Empire. It is therefore very Italian and very proud to be so. Smart Italians richly bedecked in furs and weighed down with gold come flocking here from Torino, Milano and the other cities of Lombardy. For holiday-makers from further afield, Cortina is remote and not the easiest place to get to. Most visitors, it could be argued, come to be seen. And some – perhaps the minority – come to ski.

Cortina (1230 metres; 4,035 feet), which had the distinction of hosting the Winter Olympics in 1956 (and, according to its critics, has been half-asleep ever since) has beautiful people, beautiful scenery and some of the most beautiful beginners' slopes. But it has a few tough runs too, which tend to be longer than those elsewhere in the Dolomites.

The runs (the region has forty-five blue, seventeen red and ten black) are spread around three principal skiing areas, and getting from one to the other can be a little irksome. The popular Faloria area, with the easiest access from the town centre, is loosely linked with Forcella Staunies, from which the top section of the run down is narrow, steep, stomach-churning and sometimes (mercifully) closed.

The sheer cliffs and pink hues of the Dolomites – so different from the Alps.

Opposite
There are good runs for all grades at Cortina – and cliffs for the foolhardy.

The Italians helped pioneer the high-altitude cable car, and one of these whisks you to the top where again there is no pressure actually to ski. There are almost as many good restaurants as runs. However, staying in a restaurant all day – or even sunbathing on its verandah – can have its limitations, and most of the holiday-makers who venture this far do actually make the effort eventually to ski.

There are good runs for all grades, and one great swooping run in particular through the trees down to the Passo Tre Croci (which I am assured does not mean Three Crocodile Pass) at Rio Gere. From here you can ski in the Cristallo area, which has some of the steepest runs in the Cortina locale, including one of the longest, most consistently steep descents in Europe with a huge vertical drop of 1220 metres (4,000 feet). A much easier alterna-

tive, if desired, is to take the lift back to the gentler cruising at Faloria.

By day three, most skiers are starting to move further afield and will doubtless make for the largest ski area, situated west of the town beneath the Tofana peak. This region is reached by the Freccia Nel Cielo (Arrow in the Sky) cable car.

The second stage carries skiers above the steep and craggy mountainside to Ra Valles and a beautiful and sheltered 'hidden' bowl which often enjoys excellent powder. The third and final stage hoists skiers (and the usual sprinkling of less-active visitors) almost vertically up to the pinnacle of Tofana.

Here a glass-walled restaurant offers a superb panorama of the most spectacular views across the

Cortina d'Ampezzo – Italy's answer to St Moritz.

surrounding Dolomites and meals at fairly spectacular prices. Sunbathing at 3048 metres (10,000 feet) is another popular pastime here.

These mountains are usually quite different from their neighbours in Austria. They are typically brown or coral-pink magnesian limestone topped by jagged cliffs, lending a most individual atmosphere to the skiing.

As a variant to the main Tofana skiing, you could reach the Pomedes chair lifts via Col Druscie. These provide some of Cortina's other more testing runs, including two good black runs and the exciting downhill race course. However, there is a great range of skiing on the Tofana slopes, both on- and off-piste. And in the right conditions, the area has some excellent powder skiing.

There is more. By taking a short bus ride you can link up with the famous Sella Ronda circuit (see Selva page 82). Should you wish to roam even further afield, you could purchase a Super Dolomiti ski pass which itself incorporates the Sella Ronda circuit.

Whichever route you take, you will not be very far advanced on your journey when, for some holiday-makers back in Cortina, the night life will already be under way. Indeed the apres ski starts for some at around noon. The focal point for this is the Corso Italia, where some of the 'glitterati' – ranging from aristocracy to wealthy Milanese industrialists and their offspring – take a pre-lunch stroll wearing the appropriately loud-to-garish costume and jewellery. No pretence about even planning to ski for them. They are unashamedly not going to. (Tomorrow? Perhaps.) Instead, a long lunch is planned, with lashings of Frascati or Orvieto followed by sunbathing or saying *arrivederci* to a few zillion lire in the glamorous shops until it is time to dress for dinner – preceded perhaps by a few drinks at the Piano Bar.

Then comes the inevitable discotheque/night club tour. In the Lub-Dlub disco dancing becomes a spectator sport. The Light and Laser area is surrounded by tiered seats. The Bilbao seems to attract the *nouveaux riches*. Others wander into the friendly Orange or the Hippopotinuis, which is not easy to say when your lips are cold.

I did not visit the Piano Bar, but a companion of mine did and for some reason wanted to strangle the pianist. As far as I know he did not. Had he

done so, one can imagine the immediate arrival on the scene of Inspector Clouseau – for it was in Cortina that much of the original *Pink Panther* film was shot. Should you visit the Hippopotinuis, you must judge for yourself whether the pianist deserves a reprieve.

Cortina has another most attractive attribute: it is a mere four hours from Venice. Breakfast early, then take a bus down the mountain and a train to the coast, and you can be standing by the Grand Canal waiting for the Vaporetto or enjoying a late lunch on the waterfront. Believe me, Venice in the winter months can be stunningly beautiful. The light is more Turneresque than ever. You do not have to ski every day, after all. Although with so much skiing in the Super Dolomiti area, it is tempting to keep going.

If Thomas Mann's central character in *Death in Venice* (played by Dirk Bogarde) had known about the delights of Cortina, he might have attempted the journey in reverse, slipping quietly out of Venice and cheering himself up in the resort's bubbly atmosphere.

But then perhaps this would have robbed the film of one of the world's most poignant sound tracks. The pathos of Mahler's score would have been surely inappropriate in Cortina.

SKI FACTS

RESORT HEIGHT	1230 m
RANGE	1220 – 2930 m
BLACK RUNS	8
RED RUNS	10
BLUE RUNS	32
TOTAL	50
PISTES	150 km
LIFTS	46

SELVA/ VAL GARDENA

Arizona with snow. It is not a perfect analogy by any means, but it seems to me to convey an appropriate picture of Selva/Val Gardena in the central Dolomites.

The huge, often vertical monoliths of granite that punctuate the skyline are of such gigantic proportions that the scale of the terrain comes almost as a shock for skiers only familiar with the Alps. This could be a land peopled by giants.

Carrying a camera can be time consuming and frustrating, and it should be left at home when attempting the celebrated Sella Ronda circuit otherwise you might never complete it. Exotic and surreal vistas present themselves time and time again. Sometimes both sun and moon vye for attention, splashing red and pink on to the jagged brown crags. These massifs sometimes appear so vast that they overflow the camera lens.

There is a good deal less glitter, posing and preening and a lot more emphasis on honest-to-goodness and uncompromising skiing than in Cortina. And because of its strange mixture of German and Italian influences, there is the attractive prospect of such healthy compromises as gluhwein parties at Italian prices – arguably the best of both worlds.

Although the area is dominated by chalets, the town itself is very old, with origins going back before Christ. Only a few years ago, Selva was still a poor, isolated village. The inhabitants still speak Ladin – a language derived from an original Latin dialect.

For example: *'Ula je:isa ncue:i cui schi?'* is Ladin for Where are you skiing today? (Quite how they arrived at a Ladin word for ski is a mystery to me.) The villagers earned what they could from agriculture and their famous wood carvings.

But by 1780 so many trees were being used to carve statues, altars, nativity scenes and ornaments that a decree reduced the number of carvers from three hundred to one hundred and fifty. The carvers cleverly circumvented this by buying wood from neighbouring valleys. They would travel the world – even as far afield as Russia and America – selling their wares. They came to Britain too.

Although skiers and climbers started coming here as early as 1908, tourism had to wait a long time before the local inhabitants realized it could be exploited to bring a much more prosperous lifestyle to the 'valley of the wood-carvers'. But although skiing is now flourishing, wood-carving remains an important source of revenue, and to this day many of the town's souvenir shops are overflowing with mementoes in wood.

Selva held its first downhill race in 1908 on Dantercepies and its 'Ladinia' ski club was formed in the same year. Skiers from the Gardena Valley took part in the first Olympic Games, but the real ski boom here began in the sixties and by 1970 the World Championships were being held in the resort.

Selva/Val Gardena is an early season venue for the *Ski Sunday* cameras with its World Cup race from Ciampinoi down to Santa Cristina before Christmas. This testing run was the location for the best ever World Cup performance by a British skier: Konrad Bartelski was second here in 1981.

Although the snow record is normally very good (but extremely disappointing at the start of the winter of 1988/89) the resort has installed snow-making equipment on the lower part of Saslonch, most of the Col Raiser run, the whole of Dantercepies, Risaccia. Ciampinoi and the Plan de Gralba/Piz Sella area.

It is an area which attracts mainly intermediate and advanced skiers, although there are some good beginners' slopes near the back of the village. The skiing goes up to 2950 metres (8,796 feet), and

Val Gardena is an early season venue for the World Cup downhill circuit.

there are more than ninety lifts in the Val Gardena/ Alpe di Siusi area.

Intermediates can spoil themselves on long runs back to the village – often through the trees – from the Passo Gardena. There are some wide, exhilarating runs too from Plan de Gralba and the Passo Sella, regularly punctuated by excellent mountain restaurants which the Italians fill with particularly mouth-watering fare.

Skiers can also try the famous Sella Ronda circuit and the even bigger Super Dolomiti area. This has an extraordinary number of lifts – approaching five hundred last time I tried to count them – serving well over 1,000 kilometres (620 miles) of prepared pistes on one lift pass – plus some quite outstanding scenery.

The Dolomites cover a vast area from Plan de Corones in the north to San Martino di Castrozza in the south. And from Bolzano in the west to Cortina in the east. At their heart is the great Sella massif.

This huge block of mountain is surrounded by ancient pass routes linking dozens of old villages.

The Sella Ronda circuit – which can be skied fairly comfortably (depending on queues) in a day – comprises a number of small linked resorts including Colfosco (some good nursery slopes), Corvara (open skiing, good snow), Arraba (good, testing runs) and San Cassiano (nice, easy skiing) clustering round the huge Gruppo Sella mountain, sometimes referred to as Europe's own version of Table Mountain.

It is a superbly scenic route and there are more than twenty-seven cable cars (some providing the most breathtaking rides) and bubble lifts, fifty-one chair lifts and one hundred and fifty assorted tows dotted around this hugely enjoyable ski circus.

Arizona with snow.

There are those who will tell you that the most satisfying route is clockwise. Others will insist that anti-clockwise is better. It is, as Einstein might have said, entirely relative, especially as clocks are involved.

From Selva (1563 metres; 5,128 feet) my preference is the route that delivers you to the top of the Col Rodella in time for a little fluid refreshment as the dying sun glints on the mountains – safe in the knowledge that from up here it is merely one long exhilarating schuss all the way back to Selva and a hot bath. Either way, you should leave Colfosco or Canazei (depending on which way you are skiing the circuit) at around 3.00 pm to allow plenty of time before the connecting lifts close.

There are two particularly challenging runs in Selva's own ski area. The great Forcella Sassolungo – rather picturesquely known as the 'Jaws of Death' – starts from the top of the yellow bubble lift in the Sella Pass. It is a tight, exceptionally steep run down a void of somewhat awesome proportions, and not for the faint-hearted. The run is frequently icy and sometimes dangerously rocky.

Equally steep are the black runs from the top of the nearby Sas Pordoi cable car. In fact one is so steep that a fixed rope is provided for skiers who might feel they can neither continue nor struggle back up again. This, however can have an ambivalent effect. Far from always being helpful, it can make some skiers freeze with terror as soon as they see the rope and consider its implications.

However, for those who enjoy rope-assisted descents, you can reach yet another from Pordoi. It is the start of a high-mountain tour – mainly off-piste – to Colfosco. There are some steep sections *en route* and at one rather alarming spot another rope is provided.

From Colfosco it is possible to try helicopter skiing or enjoy the runs on the huge, 3048-metre (10,000-foot) Marmolada peak or a tour through the heart of the Sella Range on the Val Mezdi. The entrance to Val Mezdi is narrow, steep and rocky and so is the final section as it brings you out into the meadows of Colfosco again.

Compared with Cortina, Selva's night life can be a shade bland and more Austrian than Italian in ambiance because of its traditional Austro-Hungarian influence (the Austrians put 8,000 Russian prisoners-of-war to work on the construction of the Val Gardena railway during the First World War). Ham hocks and dumplings are as much in evidence as pasta and peppers. Much of the area was Austrian until the end of the First World War, and to this day it is very popular with German skiers.

Most of the place names have German equivalents: Selva itself is also known as Wolkenstein, which makes it sound like a totally different place. There is even a Wolkenstein Castle – or the ruins of one – under the sheer rock face at the entrance of Vallunga. The name von Wolkenstein was adopted by the owner in 1291. In 1380 the Lords of Wolkenstein moved to Trotsburg Castle, above Ponte Gardena. By 1525 the castle was in ruins and has never been restored. Gardena Castle, however – owned by a Venetian baron – has been restored and is a splendid building, especially when floodlit.

The valley has a magical feeling about it, and no matter how you spend your day or where you ski, then chances are that by sunset, when the stupendous massifs catch the dying rays, you will be saying '*I ie sta n bel di*' – it has been a beautiful day.

And even Einstein would not argue with that.

SKI FACTS

RESORT HEIGHT	1550 m
RANGE	1225 – 2950 m
BLACK RUNS	2
RED RUNS	18
BLUE RUNS	11
TOTAL	31
PISTES	175 km
LIFTS	75

ANDERMATT

The fearsome Gemsstock.

Andermatt is the half-forgotten, neglected gem of the Swiss Alps, a little jaded and unpolished of late – but one feels that it could so easily be rescued from the doldrums, dusted down and made to shine again.

It certainly used to shine. My wonderfully battered and ancient *Baedeker's Switzerland* (1909) describes it as 'a health resort in summer and a centre of sports in winter.' The guide also mentions, in passing, Andermatt's artillery camp. With hindsight, eighty years later, the seeds of neglect were already there. It was the army's early presence which was to change the course of this beautiful resort's history.

Hardly any British tour operators go there any more. And yet it was once one of the most popular destinations for British skiers. I even put on my first pair of skis there on a school trip when I was sixteen. I did not ski again for fourteen years, so it should have been firmly etched in my mind as my first love affair with skiing – complete with the inevitable cable bindings, leather boots and skis as long as your outstretched arm. Yet I almost forgot to include it in this book.

The reason for Andermatt's relative obscurity these days is that the skiing there has virtually been taken over by the Swiss army for training purposes. So foreign tourists do not get much of a look in. For the same reason, the lift system has not made a great deal of progress since the sixties because the present set-up is quite adequate for the guaranteed army 'clientelle.'

The village, at 1444 metres (4,737 feet) in the Urserental is still most attractive (apart from the barracks) and it all seems rather a waste of a good resort, although the army must be delighted to have the place pretty much to themselves.

The reason I am keen to include it in my selection of the world's best is not a sentimental one, however. Having started my skiing 'career'

here, I knew little of the 'grown-up' skiing available.

Recently I returned to Andermatt to join the renowned Martin Epp on a ski tour – climbing on 'skins' (once genuine animal skins but now strips of nylon substitute) for most of the day before skiing down to the next mountain hut and repeating the whole performance the following day, rarely descending from the mountains into a village until the tour was completed.

As I had anticipated, this tour served to confirm what I had heard: that there is some exciting and tough skiing above Andermatt – particularly on the famous and sometimes frightening Gemsstock (2743 metres; 9,000 feet) – which makes it a top resort even though comparatively few foreign skiers are able to take advantage of it. Most recreational skiers here are the Swiss themselves and the Italians.

It is the runs down the front of the Gemsstock which give Andermatt its somewhat fearsome reputation. The vertical drop of almost 760 metres (2,500 feet) is nearly all pretty severe, much of it

off-piste, and some of it avalanche-prone. For this reason a guide is an extremely good idea, especially for the long off-piste descents to Hospental and Andermatt.

There is considerably easier skiing at Nätschen, Hospental and Realp, and the run from Nätschen to Andermatt I remember with particular affection from my days as a young beginner.

Andermatt's position in the district of Uri is unusually central. It is only a few kilometres from three more of Switzerland's cantons: the Grisons, Ticino and Valaise (via the Oberalp, Gotthard and Furka passes). Indeed it is the tourist office's proud boast that in one day you can 'eat ossobuco

Andermatt: once a paradise for British children. It still is for the locals, though the Swiss army has stamped its authority on the resort.

Ticinerse, raclette with Valaisan bread and barley soup from the Grisons.' For this reason it is sometimes referred to as being at the crossroads of the Alps. By climbing the Gemsstock, you can actually see all these regions – and a lot more. A startlingly high number of peaks – six hundred in all – are said to be visible from the summit.

But for the army, I suspect that by now Andermatt would be one of the most famous resorts in Europe instead of languishing in the doldrums. Even the Swiss tourist office is sad at the way things have gone there. Hopefully one day it will bounce back. I would love to be there if it does.

SKI FACTS

RESORT HEIGHT	1444 m
RANGE	1444 – 2963 m
BLACK RUNS	7
RED RUNS	5
BLUE RUNS	5
TOTAL	17
PISTES	55 km
LIFTS	12

Andermatt: a forgotten gem, with some magnificent skiing.

DAVOS/Klosters

So this is where it all started. Well, at least one of the places. Davos is of course not the only resort where skiing was pioneered, but it boasts more than its fair share of skiing innovations.

The world's first tow bar was built here by a young German engineer called Gerhard Mueller with the help of a rope and some motorcycle parts. Then in 1931 came the first funicular for skiers up to the Weissfluhjoch. From here skiers could return to Davos, ski to Klosters or take the famous Parsenn run down to Kublis. And in 1934 Erich Constam built the world's first 'proper' drag lift.

Even before the turn of the century, however, a celebrated holiday-maker made history when he became the first Englishman to undertake a tour on skis – or 'ski' as they were quaintly referred to at the time. 'Ski' he concluded, 'are the most capricious things upon earth. One day you cannot go wrong with them. On another, with the same weather and the same snow, you cannot go right.'

The words are those of Sir Arthur Conan Doyle, whose description of one of the very first journeys over the Furka Pass from Davos to Arosa – told in *Strand* magazine in 1894 – makes fascinating reading but would doubtless today fall foul of the race relations board. 'The first time you try to turn' he writes, 'the great "ski" flapping in the air has the queerest appearance, like an exaggerated nigger dance.'

The creator of Sherlock Holmes was the first Englishman to undertake a mountain tour 'on ski.' With him were two Swiss guides.

'You adjust your body for a rapid slide' he wrote, 'but your "ski" stick motionless, and over you go upon your face. Then you stop upon the level, and have just time to say: "What a lovely view is this!" when you find yourself standing on your two shoulder blades with your "ski" tied tightly round your neck.

'Or you stop for an instant to tell a group . . . how well you are getting on . . . and they suddenly find that their congratulations are addressed to the soles of your "ski." '

Picture-postcard scenery around Davos – a town with a permanent population of 15,000 people.

Opposite
Klosters's own ski area, the Gotschnagrat.

Conan Doyle was not put off by such embarrassing episodes however, and made a forecast of Holmesian astuteness: 'I am convinced' he wrote, 'that the time will come when hundreds of Englishmen will come to Switzerland for the "ski"-ing season.'

Davos, which at 1560 metres (5,118 feet) claims to be Europe's highest big town, was an appropriate location for this glimpse into the future. Like St Moritz, Davos was famous as a winter health resort long before sliding on 'ski' became popular. The first English ski club was also founded here in 1903 (the same year as the Ski Club of Great Britain was launched).

Just like St Moritz, Davos's rise to fame and popularity was quick and dramatic. In the winter of 1866, there were *two* visitors. By 1874 there were more than three hundred, most of them English, and most of them convalescing, as often as not, from tuberculosis. Some of the best hotels here were once clinics. (According to *Baedeker's Switzerland* (1909) the air in Davos 'is remarkably pure and dry.')

Even in one of Europe's busiest ski towns you can still escape.

Invalids or not, they were determined to have a good time. And in Davos, that usually meant toboganing. By 1883, Davos had its own Tobog-ganing Club, and held a competition against St Moritz.

It was not until 1883 that the first pair of skis appeared in Davos. A German schoolboy there was given a pair by his Norwegian tutor.

Raymond Flower, in his profile of St Moritz, *The Palace*, describes how the skis were copied by the village carpenter, and 'a few of the local lads could be seen staggering about with curious planks on their feet – but none of them had any idea how to use them.' Later two English brothers – the Richardsons – also acquired some Norwegian skis, and practised on them on the slopes near the church.

Dame Katherine Furse, who later became President of the British Ladies Ski Club, also had problems when she was given her first pair in Davos. With her soft shoes, she had no control, and could neither run nor turn on them. Without wax, the snow also tended to stick to the skis. 'All this was somewhat discouraging' she confessed.

'We tended to look on the ski as a toy rather than as a useful means of progression.' As it turns out, she was wrong, and Davos today has some of the best skiing in Switzerland – and the country's largest ski school.

The focal point – most of which is shared with its much smaller but more exclusive neighbour Klosters – is the famous Parsennalp. With the Weissfluh this area at 2834 metres (9,300 feet) links with Shatzalp-Strela, above Davos Platz and the Klosters Gotschna ski area, and is served by three cable cars and at least half a dozen drag lifts.

This is the location of one of the most celebrated descents in Switzerland – the Parsenn 'Derby' run down to Klosters which most competent skiers will enjoy immensely. It is a long thirteen kilometres (eight miles) but not particularly difficult.

There are five skiing areas altogether in the Davos/Klosters region, with more than 322 kilometres (200 miles) of pistes between them. There is also some wonderful off-piste skiing.

The Jakobshorn-Bramabüel area at 2590 metres and 2476 metres (8,500 feet and 8,126 feet) has some excellent skiing above the tree-line with an eight-kilometre (five-mile) run back to Davos. And there is some very attractive skiing down Dorftalli and Meierhofer Talli.

If you take the train to Davos Glaris, you reach the excellent skiing area called the Rinerhorn at 2490 metres (8,170 feet). This has a good mixture of all grades of skiing, with some exhilarating off-piste descents off the back (take a guide).

The sunniest areas are probably at Madrisa and Pischa, in the Fluella Valley (with lifts going up to 2485 metres; 8,153 feet) where it is warm and wide and ideal for beginners.

Klosters, thirteen kilometres (eight miles) away and 1200 metres (3,937 feet) up in the Prattigau Valley is traditionally frequented by the rich and the royal. It has its own unusual and beautiful skiing area around the Gotschnagrat.

The best route back from Davos – via Gotschnagrat – is arguably the Drostobel run. The off-piste run from the top section under the cable car incorporates the fearsome and notorious Gotschnawang descent (known locally simply as the Wang run – Wang meaning steep slope) close to where Prince Charles's party was so tragically overwhelmed by an avalanche in 1988.

Ironically this happened only a comparatively short distance from the Weissfluhjoch Avalanche Research centre set up by Swiss scientists to study avalanche patterns and snow conditions. They also monitor the weather and send out warnings about unsafe areas all over Switzerland.

Apart from the extensive ski area of Davos and Klosters, the resorts are surrounded by magnificent touring country. Beyond Klosters is the famous Silvretta range in Austria.

The simple way to get the best of both Davos and Klosters, it seems to me, is to stay in delightful Klosters and ski – and if necessary, shop – in Davos. You might have a slightly livelier time by staying in Davos, but it is, after all, a town, and personally I would much rather sleep in a cosy traditional Alpine village than in just another Zurich or Montreux.

And who knows – you might just catch a glimpse of Prince Charles. His annual visit to Klosters is undoubtedly one of the major therapeutic influences in his life. It is certainly a beautiful spot – and a far cry from the problems of crumbling inner cities. He would doubtless like to take Klosters, and the wonderful mountains that surround it, home to Britain and add it to his kingdom.

SKI FACTS

RESORT HEIGHT	1560 m
RANGE	1127 – 2844 m
BLACK RUNS	26
RED RUNS	36
BLUE RUNS	26
TOTAL	88
PISTES	270 km
LIFTS	36

GRINDELWALD/ WENGEN/Mürren

The first intoxicating, mesmerizing look at that extraordinary trio of peaks, the Eiger, Mönch and Jungfrau is so startling that one can hardly believe one's eyes. Like the Matterhorn or Wyoming's Teton range, their beauty and huge physical presence almost defy credulity.

In more than one sense Grindelwald, at the base of the Eiger (Ogre) which shoots up from the meadows, lives in Wengen's shadow. Tucked away in a steep-sided though extremely beautiful valley the village itself receives little sunshine, whereas its smaller neighbour, basking on a wide-open terrace below the Jungfrau, can be sunny all day.

The British love Wengen (a corruption of Wang or Wangen, a local dialect which means a steep slope). Indeed, they practically invented the place, and the passion – eccentric at the time – for winter sports. Sir Arnold Lunn set the first modern slalom course on the slopes at Mürren, on the other side of the Lauterbrunnen Valley, in 1922.

Wengen at 1274 metres (4,180 feet) is the home of the celebrated Down Hill Only club (DHO) – so called because when the Swiss started building the delightful cog mountain railways over a century ago, there were no such things as chair lifts, and the trains represented a wonderful new alternative to slogging up the mountain carrying your skis or walking up on them with seal skins on the bottom to stop you sliding backwards. So eventually – in the twenties – the triumphant British started to leap aboard the trains and ski 'downhill only'.

Even today the train enables skiers to indulge themselves in a way that is impossible in other resorts. You can use them as an 'after-hours' ski lift once the official ones have closed. It is a delicious feeling – a mixture of exhilaration and schoolboy mischief – to hurtle down to Wengen or Grund station at the end of the day, climb on board the train, and enjoy one last run down from Kleine Scheidegg, sometimes in twilight or even moonlight! This practice is not encouraged by the authorities –

and should you be careless enough to have an accident they and your insurance company would almost certainly wash their hands of you. Yet I did discover to my satisfaction that on nights when there is a fullish moon, the locals themselves sometimes indulge in a spot of moonlight skiing.

DHO members are very faithful to Wengen. Some have been back year after year to this charming, (almost) traffic-free village and would never venture anywhere else. Wives come too – even if they do not ski. They seem content to while away the weeks – even months – just enjoying life in such picturesque surroundings, while their husbands ski the same old runs they may have originally tackled on hickory skis with cable bindings and old leather boots.

'But why don't you try a different resort?' I asked one crusty old gentleman. 'Never' he said. 'Like to know what's round the next corner.' This, I thought, was the club for me. 'How does one join?' I asked. 'Well old boy' he said, 'first of all you've got to be the right sort of chap.' That probably ruled me out instantly. 'Then you have to go and ski with one of our members . . . You go up to the top of the mountain.' (Any mountain would do, apparently.) 'I light a cigar, you ski down – and if my cigar's still alight when you get down – you're in!' I did join. But he never did light that cigar.

Needless to say, Wengen has not always been so affluent. When the first 'tourists' arrived early in the last century, it was only to pass through the 'impoverished and sleepy farming hamlet' on their way to the much more sought-after village of Grindelwald. But somehow a little of Grindelwald's early popularity rubbed off on its neighbour, and Wengen's first guest house opened in 1859. The building of the region's first mountain railway, the

Ski-touring in the Jungfrau region.

Wengernalpbahn, in the 1880s virtually guaranteed that Wengen would secure its own little place on the map alongside its rival.

Wengen has been around for at least 721 years, and there is a fascinating mystery story associated with it which Sir Arnold Lunn refers to in his book *The Bernese Oberland*. It concerns the village of Rubenstand, which Lunn picturesquely describes as 'The Alpine equivalent of Atlantis.' Its location is thought to be near the Schlafbühel on the Wengernalp. 'There is no written record of the village' writes Lunn, 'but there are still traces on the Schlafbühel of a path which once led to a vanished Catholic chapel.' Not even the most senior members of the DHO seem able to recall the village.

Lunn also mentions another legendary village – Z'Gassen, the site of present-day Gassenboden where mineral implements have been found, left behind by Celtic miners.

The Bernese Oberland, and especially Grindelwald, was one of the most fashionable locations for touring celebrities: Byron, Shelley, Thackeray, Ruskin, Matthew Arnold, Brahms, Turner, Mark Twain and even Queen Victoria are documented visitors.

Byron's play *Manfred* is said to have been inspired by his crossing of the Scheidegg in 1816. He describes the glaciers above Grindelwald as 'a frozen hurricane.' In *Manfred*, Byron speaks of 'The glassy ocean of the mountain ice ... a tumbling tempest's foam, frozen in a moment.'

And Virginia Woolf's father, the writer Leslie Stephen eulogized about Wengernalp thus in a letter to Sir Arnold Lunn, the 'father' of slalom skiing: 'To me the Wengern Alp is a sacred place – the holy of holies in the mountain sanctuary, and the emotions produced when no desecrating influence is present and old memories rise up, are softened by the sweet sadness of the scenery.'

And in his *Playground of Europe*, Stephen writes: 'If I were to invent a new idolatry I should prostrate myself not before beast, or ocean or sun but before one of those gigantic masses to which ... it is impossible not to attribute some shadowy personality.'

He was not the first to characterize the famous trio of Eiger, 3972 metres (13,033 feet), Mönch, 4100 metres (13,449 feet) and Jungfrau, 4158 metres (13,642 feet) whose very names conjure up visions of an Ogre, Monk and a young and virginal maiden. Skiing beneath this trio in the Wengen/ Grindlewald area on a sunny day is little short of perfection. It may not be the most exciting skiing in the world (my usual criterion for a good resort) but the endless joyful red runs, gorgeous scenery, and sunny days create the most charming and blissful atmosphere where almost any skier would have to be an extremely miserable soul not to experience a genuine *joie de vivre*.

But while everyone is joy-riding on skis through this vale of plenty in near idyllic circumstances, there can be events in chilling contrast taking place above them – on the North Face of one of Europe's fiercest mountains, the Eiger.

During one of my many recent visits to the area that contrast was at its most extreme. I discovered after a perfect day's skiing – with scarcely a care in the world that had not been playfully blown away by the euphoria of it all – that two Korean climbers had disappeared on the Eiger's most merciless face. They were up there, somewhere – frozen to the mountainside, while we were all enjoying the equivalent of a winter picnic below.

The focal point of this strange dichotomy is the railway. The Jungfraubahn (Europe's highest rack railway) curls up to the Jungfraujoch (3454 metres (11,332 feet) – Europe's highest railway station) in most dramatic fashion – through the very North Face of the Eiger itself. *En route* it halts at two extraordinary stations where passengers are allowed five minutes to peer out of the windows at what must be one of the most chilling sights in Europe.

Ogre, monk and maiden – better known as the Eiger, Mönch and Jungfrau.

Opposite
Wengen – surrounded by some of the most stunning scenery in the Alps.

Above and below is the frighteningly sheer North Face itself, with huge jagged rocks topped with wild cornices. You are in it, part of it, yet, like a scientist looking through the glass screen separating him from a nuclear reaction, strangely safe from its terrors. Near the windows are doors through which some of the most dramatic, heroic and heart-rending rescue attempts on the terrible North Face have been attempted.

Having withdrawn from this astonishing scene, you continue by train to the top, from which unrolls one of the greatest glaciers in the world, the Aletsch. In 1909, before the Jungfrau section of the mountain railway had been constructed, Sir Arnold Lunn undertook the first end-to-end ski traverse of the Oberland from Kandersteg to Meiringen.

His party saw the tracks of other skiers in the snow, and he wrote in his book *The Bernese Oberland*: 'Some afterglow from the flame of speed still seemed to linger . . . some lingering echo of the hiss of powder snow in the banked curves thrown up by their ski.' Making their own tracks, Lunn wrote:

As the ski cut round, the superficial film of soft ice fell away and rippled down the slope with a sound like the soft splash of a glacier stream, an underlying melody that disputed the bolder music of the wind.

We set our ski for a straight run. We crouched down, the wind sang its last song ... the breeze died away, four rapid swings and four breathless skirunners faced the slope whose swift joys they had squandered all too soon.

Also at the Junfraujoch is a permanently manned observatory, and a most exotic ice 'palace' where you walk through a maze of ice corridors. Every now and them you encounter superb ice sculpture in alcoves and recesses. During my last visit – early in 1989 – there was a Japanese flavour to celebrate one hundred years of winter sports in the region in 1988. More Japanese tourists visit Grindelwald than any other Swiss resort, and they marvelled at the sculptures of Buddha, a pagoda, a hotel and all manner of other carefully crafted blocks of ice – even a car.

Kleine Scheidegg and its neighbour Männlichen, the high pivotal plateau of the Wengen/Grindelwald ski area, are, like Grindelwald itself, a traditional location for watching great Eiger exploits, and sometimes, terrible tragedies through the inevitable binoculars or telescope. If you look carefully, even with the unaided eye, you can just make out the famous station windows through which you have already peered from Eigerwand station.

Hiding right beneath the North Face is one of Wengen's very best off-piste areas. You would never realize it existed unless you were taken there, and because of avalanche dangers it is advisable to take a guide or instructor with you.

You reach the area from the Eigergletscher, and traverse a quarter of a mile or so until – although you cannot see it – you are almost directly above the Salzegg area.

Then you climb for about fifteen minutes, carrying your skis before reaching a smallish dip almost at the very foot of the North Face. You feel you could reach out and touch the dreaded 'White Spider' which has trapped and killed so many fine young climbers. (Once climbers reach this spine-chilling part of the mountain, there is said to be no direction in which to move but up. Descent is impossible.)

Beneath you is a wonderful powder run known as the White Hare. There are two sections which together will enable you to make as many as a hundred turns. In a resort not noted for its off-piste skiing, this is something of a treat. If you enjoy the White Hare, you will also be pleased by the Oh God! run, down to Wixi, and the steep black descent called Black Rock. Like White Hare, both are reached from Eigergletscher.

If you include neighbouring Mürren, famous for its Kandahar Club and Schilthorn, crowned with the revolving restaurant which featured in the James Bond film, *On Her Majesty's Secret Service*, the Jungfrau Region has over 160 kilometres (100 miles) of skiing.

Mürren has some excellent off-piste skiing, but apart from the Schilthorn and the famous descent used for the Inferno race, the piste-skiing in Mürren is somewhat limited, and the main skiing in the region is shared between Wengen and Grindelwald at 1036 metres (3,400 feet), the largest of the Bernese Oberland ski resorts.

Grindelwald is traditionally more of a climbing village than a ski resort, but it has its own ski area at First (pronounced Fierce) with one of those wonderfully antiquated wooden chair lifts with a canvas roof that travels up the mountain sideways.

The lift, in four sections, is said to be the longest in Europe. But it is due to be replaced – at last – by a gondola sometime around 1990. (I shall quite miss the original – it was like an old fairground ride.)

Grindelwald has the most stunning view of the Wetterhorn at 3703 metres (12,149 feet), Schreckhorn at 4080 metres (13,385 feet) and of course the Eiger.

The Schreckhorn is known by some local inhabitants as the 'Peak of Dread', and in the Middle Ages the two snow slopes near the summit were associated with the imprisoned souls of two nuns from a convent at Interlaken who broke their vows.

'First' is a large sunny, wide-open, south-facing area with quite a bit of skiing above the tree-line. One run in particular is long and occasionally quite challenging – from the Oberjoch back down to Grindelwald. The eight-kilometre (five-mile) descent has a vertical drop of 1524 metres (5,000 feet).

Mürren – a quaint, historical resort which has changed little since Sir Henry Lunn brought the first tourists to the area over seventy years ago.

In spite of its size, Grindelwald – surrounded by spectacular glaciers – is a most pretty place, full of traditional wooden buildings. Like Mürren, it too has an English hero to thank for its early pioneering days of skiing, but he pre-dates Arnold Lunn by many years. According to the tourist office literature:

> The first skier, an Englishman named Gerald Fox, appeared 1881. He fastened his skis already in the hotel room. He put his long stick in the snow and glide away. In squatting vauld he glided down the slope, the wooden stick like a folding boat balancing.

The good Mr Fox, it seems, was the precursor of many distinguished visitors who 'pilgrim to the classical skiregion, flit over the slopes . . . or stroll respectful or calm underneath the mammoth north wall of the Eiger.'

Wengen's most famous run is the celebrated Lauberhorn, the longest, and one of the greatest and most scenic World Cup downhill courses.

Mürren is host to one of the most astonishing ski races in Europe, the famous Inferno down the Schilthorn (3066 metres; 10,059 feet) with its famous – often mogul-packed – 'Kanonenrohr' section all the way down to Lauterbrunnen (796 metres; 2,611 feet). It is said to be the longest downhill race in the world. Every January more than 1,400 skiers attempt it, including some fairly average skiers. I was privileged to take part in it with my friend Neil English during the winter of 1988/89 when Peter Lunn – son of Sir Arnold and once one of Britain's finest racers – took part for the last time (or so he said).

A novel means of exploring the terrain below the Jungfraujoch.

The record time for the complete descent (there are shortened versions when the snow is poor at the bottom) is just under sixteen minutes. But many participents take much longer. A colleague – whom I shall not embarrass by naming – took over an hour, although sixty years ago this would have been no disgrace!

The race was inaugurated on 29th January 1928. First home was Harold Mitchell in 1 hour 12 minutes. 'Deggers (A H d'Egville) and I were 6th' said Lunn later. The following year, a wonderful character called Jimmy Riddell (yes, he *is* a little tired of the jokes) won it. Riddell tells wonderful stories about Sir Arnold Lunn and his chums in the Kandahar Club pioneering 'slalom' skiing in Mürren – as opposed to langlauf (cross-country) or ski-jumping.

Norwegian hickory 'ski' in those days – fitted with steel edges, or brass if you could afford them – were available for around three guineas from Harrods. With them you could purchase a 'snow-proof, zipp-waisted ski suit' for seven guineas.

During the Arnold Lunn centenary celebrations at Mürren in the winter of 1988/89, Jimmy Riddell told me how they had all emptied the feathers from duvets to create make-believe 'snow' at the Hotel Alpina and organized a ski race down the hotel staircase. Crazy, heady days!

On 30th January 1924 – more than a year before the DHO was formed across the valley in Wengen – Lunn founded the Kandahar Club. It was named after General Lord Roberts of Kandahar, Afghanistan, who had donated a silver chalice as a prize for Sir Henry Lunn's skiing guests. The first downhill team race in skiing history had been held on the Grindelwald slopes of the Scheidegg. Among the racers were Wengeners, who, according to Dr Zahnd, the Kurdirector of Wengen, 'learned from the British not only to race and to battle but also to lose.'

With the possible exception of Zermatt, the Wengen/Grindelwald/Mürren area must be regarded as the most beautiful scenery in Switzerland. It is the very essence of Switzerland – and a visit there either on skis or off, in winter or summer, is an unforgettable experience. Sir Arnold Lunn found the view from the revolving restaurant at the top of Mürren's Schilthorn particularly emotional. It was a poignant location for a man who – when young –

certainly had no cable cars to help him reach the heights. Yet now he found himself effortlessly transported to the peaks he adored, and the experience moved him to write with great emotion:

The mountains have given me of their best and now that I can no longer climb, I assumed that I could not hope for any new mountain experience. I was wrong. As the revolving restaurant carried me slowly from the Lauberhorn, the first mountain that I had ever climbed, as a boy of six, to the Aiguille du Gouter in the far-off Mont Blanc range, my last peak, which I climbed at the age of sixty-eight, I felt as if I were travelling through time, as if time were indeed a fourth dimension in which I could freely move . . . I have never, since they died, felt nearer to the beloved companions with whom I had climbed and skied than in that memorable hour.

SKI FACTS

RESORT HEIGHT	Wengen 1274 m
	Grindelwald 1034 m
RANGE	1943 – 2971 m
BLACK RUNS	10
RED RUNS	25
BLUE RUNS	18
TOTAL	63
PISTES	176 km
LIFTS	43
LONGEST RUN	10 km

GSTAAD

A mong the many celebrities who favour Gstaad and its beautiful surroundings is, we are told, the biggest VIP of them all. Not Roger Moore. God. How do we know this? The local tourist office tells us with great confidence. In their publicity material, we learn the following fascinating fact:

> After God created the world, he wished to make one more exceptional landscape. He pressed his hand on earth like a personal autograph and the lovely Saanenland was born. The thumb imprint is Saanenmöser, the forefinger is Turbachtal, the middle and the ring finger formed the valleys of the Lauibach and Saane, and the little finger represented the Chalberhoni.

With God on Gstaad's side, what need of mere kings? But then – also according to the gospel of the Gstaad tourist office: 'In Gstaad, every guest is a king, but kings are only guests.' A nice slogan and a fair assessment of what the locals would like their image to be. Kings, however, might not quite see it that way. But with or without kings, Gstaad is difficult to ignore.

Some resorts are great because of their exciting and picturesque skiing – which is the way I like them. Others simply cannot be overlooked because of their reputation. Reputations come and go, of course, but good mountains tend to linger on.

However, somehow Gstaad – nestling at 1097 metres (3,600 feet) in the Saane/Sarine valley between the Bernese Oberland and Lake Geneva – has captured a certain glamorous image which makes it very difficult to omit from the world's best, even though its own ski areas (Eggli, Wispile and Wasserngrat) are not the most exciting in the world in spite of Divine planning. But if you add

Silent night.

in the surrounding skiing areas – the Gstaad Superski Region – scattered around its environs and its satellites, the skiing (250 kilometres (155 miles) of it served by more than seventy lifts) starts to become interesting.

Whether these regions – Rougemont, Saanen, Schönried, Zweisimmen and St Stephan – actually enjoy basking in the 'glory' of Gstaad or would prefer a separate identity of their own I found difficult to establish during my last visit. Apart from other considerations there is a language change – Rougemont, as one might assume, is French speaking, while in Gstaad, equally obviously, the natives (yes, there are a few left in spite of the influx of foreign millionaires) speak German.

Gstaad, like Wengen owes much of its initial prosperity to the arrival of the mountain railway soon after the turn of the century. But unlike Wengen, St Moritz, Davos, and indeed all the major Swiss resorts, Gstaad is the only one which did not spring up through the Anglo-Saxon connection – the fashion by Englishmen and women of summering and then wintering in the Alps.

Quite why the English did not flock here is unclear. Gstaad is undeniably pretty and even more undeniably expensive. Those in the know suggest that you do not have to be seriously rich to live in St Moritz, but no such wild claims are made for Gstaad. Quite simply, you do. Everything from the famous and luxurious Palace Hotel (which dominates the skyline) down to the small hotels, chalets and apartments is expensive – the Palace extremely so.

Sadly, the arrival of a *nouveau riche* society (many of whom would scarcely know one end of a ski from another, let alone ever actually put a pair on) has brought with it something almost unthinkable for a Swiss mountain village – crime.

Much of it is hushed up by the local press, whose attitudes are rather different from their British counterparts. Crime is as dirty a word in a fashionable ski resort as avalanche. As often as not, details of the odd smash and grab raid or the occasional avalanche death do not feature in Swiss newspapers.

The most demanding skiing in Gstaad itself is on the Wasserngrat, close to whose peak is the Eagle Club, the world-famous and extremely exclusive luncheon club. Parts of Wispile are also testing, while Eggli provides much of the gentler and sunnier skiing.

Elsewhere, there is some exciting stuff high on the Diablerets glacier (at just under 3048 metres; 10,000 feet), shared with the resort of Les Diablerets and Videmanette above Rougemont (especially at the top where the degree of difficulty can become quite dramatic in some conditions). With good powder the off-piste skiing can be superb.

There is also floodlit skiing in Rougemont – an idea that is becoming popular in many American resorts where businessmen cannot find time in the day to ski. The skiing at Saanenmoser is a delightful area of considerable interest to intermediates and improving novices.

Without for a moment wishing to be sacriligious, the Almighty did a good job here – but perhaps had he foreseen man's strange yearning to slide down his mountains on planks, he might have planned things slightly differently, and made the skiing a little more exciting.

SKI FACTS

RESORT HEIGHT	1100 m
RANGE	1100 – 3000 m
BLACK RUNS	7
RED RUNS	26
BLUE RUNS	24
TOTAL	57
PISTES	250 km
LIFTS	69

GSTAAD
✦ 1000-3000 m
SUPER SKI REGION

ST MORITZ

St Moritz, at 1856 metres (6,089 feet) in the magnificent Engadine Valley is the most famous winter sports resort in the world.

It immediately conjures up images of the hooves of race-horses pounding across the frozen lake, men of steel hurling themselves down the infamous Cresta run, and elegant, lavishly scented and fur-coated women and dinner-jacketed men savouring a luxurious meal at the celebrity-packed Palace Hotel or haunting casinos filled with swirling cigar smoke and the triple intoxication of money, power and expensive cocktails.

Located at a cultural crossroads, where three different languages mingle – Romantsch, Italian and German – some kind of primitive settlement existed in St Moritz as long ago as 3000 BC. And like so many winter sports resorts, it originally became popular as a spa – one of the world's earliest. By the time the Romans conquered the region in 15 BC the settlement was well known for the so-called health-giving red waters that trickled out of Piz Rosatch. The waters were also taken by crusaders and merchants travelling over the Julier and Splugen during their journeys across the Alps.

By 1537 the physician Theophrastus Bombastus von Hohenheim had noted that

> . . . of all the mineral springs in Europe . . . the one I prize the highest is at Sankt Mauritz. Whoever drinks this water . . . will never become acquainted with either stone or gravel, gout or arthritis; his stomach will be strengthened so that he can digest acid like an ostrich digests a piece of iron . . .

Later 'patients' however, complained that the water tasted like ink, and made them feel light-headed and exhausted.

St Moritz gets its name from the cult of St Mauritius – a third century Theban commander who was massacred with his men for refusing to persecute Christians.

By 1841, there was still nothing exclusive about the place. Rodolphe Topfer, a French writer, described the locals as 'a grotesque mixture of heady peasants, idle gentry, tipplers, makers of cheese and of cannons at billiards.'

All this changed in 1864 after the now celebrated wager made by Johannes Badrutt (grandfather of the present owner of The Palace), who then owned the Kulm Hotel. In those days tourists only came to the mountains in the summer. It was September, and time for the English tourists to go home. According to Raymond Flower, in his history of

After a hard day's skiing . . . dusk in the magnificent Engadine.

Below
Not quite St Andrews – but at least the nineteenth hole serves gluhwein.

the celebrated Palace Hotel, the conversation went like this:

> True, winter is just around the corner. But do you know that the winter here is much more pleasant and a good deal less cold than in London? Do you realize that on sunny days it is so warm that we go about in shirt-sleeves?

Badrutt then made his famous invitation:

> I would like to offer you the chance of checking my statement for yourselves. This winter you shall be my guests at the Kulm. You will not pay anything for your stay. I bet that you will agree that what I have said is true.

If they did not, Badrutt promised to pay their travelling expenses. The Englishmen could not lose.

They duly arrived, remained for the entire winter – and more – and an entry in the visitors' book records: 'Far from finding it cold, the heat of the sun is so intense at times that sunshades were indispensable. The brilliance of the sun, the blueness of the sky and the clearness of the atmosphere quite surprised us.' As Flower observes: 'The concept of a winter sports holiday had been born. It was to change the face of St Moritz.' Not to mention the entire Alps.

By 1876, a *Times* reader who had spent the winter at the Kulm was reporting:

> We were to perish with cold owing to the insufficient means of warming the rooms.

Skiing, in those early days, was still scornfully dismissed by the inhabitants of St Moritz as 'plank hopping'. Throughout the twenties skating remained the dominant activity there. By 1909, *Baedeker's Switzerland* was recording that winter guests in St Moritz now numbered 2,000 – 'most are English (no consumptives)!'

It was the 1928 Winter Olympics that changed all that. With them came the new ratchet railway linking Corviglia with Chanterella – built, astonishingly, in a single summer (eight months) by three hundred workers, which opened up the snow fields between Corviglia and Alp Giop. (This and the cable car were rebuilt and re-opened four years ago amid a fanfare of verbal trumpets.) Plank hopping had become respectable. Skiing had come to stay. Nowadays you can ski in almost every possible way in St Moritz – even by being towed across the ice by a horse! (Ski-joring.)

In 1935, the first lift opened on Suvretta (only the second ski lift to be built in Switzerland), and three years later came the Corviglia cable car. In 1948, St Moritz hosted the fifth Winter Olympics. By January, 1955, a cable car was transporting skiers to the top of Piz Nair, at more than 3048 metres (10,000 feet). The following year, the cable car to the magnificent Diavolezza glacier was inaugurated, which opened up some of the most exciting skiing in Switzerland.

Later, one of the most famous and rich among the hordes of celebrities who regularly wintered in St Moritz – Stavros Niarchos – helped pioneer the concept of helicopter skiing in which you use a helicopter as your own personal ski-lift to the cream of the unpisted slopes. He helped finance a new cable car from Corviglia at 2438 metres (8,000 feet) to Piz Nair at 3048 metres (10,000 feet) and lent his name to the superb steep run down its

But when does Christmas in England see village windows gay with flowers? Here geraniums, lobelias, cinerarias, fuchsias, marigolds and roses in full bloom attest the even temperature of the humblest dwelling rooms.

Within a few short years, St Moritz was to grow from an 'undistinguished hamlet into an international resort.'

Oddly enough, every kind of winter sport *except* skiing was practised in St Moritz. Skating and tobogganing were the popular sports, and a great rivalry developed with Davos which involved numerous inter-resort tobogganing races, and led to the construction of the soon-to-be-famous snow-banked track down the gully between St Moritz and the little hamlet of Cresta.

St Moritz can boast some first-rate off-piste skiing.

north face. And in the sixties, he backed the new complex of cable cars and restaurants up to Corvatsch at 3450 metres (11,320 feet) which helped St Moritz to become one of the most extensive skiing areas in Europe. In the winter of 1972/73, a new cable car was built to Signal, linking St Moritz Bad with Corviglia.

My first glimpse of St Moritz – and it was scarcely more than a glimpse – was as a totally over-awed refugee from a former Italian penal colony now masquerading as a ski resort called Livigno. As an advancing and fairly foolhardy beginner, I had taken advantage of an opportunity offered to myself and other punters to enjoy a major treat – a journey by mini-bus over the mountain pass from one of the least consequential ski resorts in Europe to the most prestigious.

It was the skiing equivalent of travelling from Rotherham to the Ritz for a slap-up meal. (Mini-buses are not the most fashionable way to arrive in St Moritz. You can take the Glacier Express or even fly in direct from Zurich.)

At luck would have it, St Moritz, which normally enjoys a superb climate was immersed in a near-total white-out, and my skiiing companion and

fellow-refugee, Paul, and myself appeared to be the only people on Corviglia. But this was to be our one and only chance of skiing for the first time in this legendary resort, and whatever the weather, we were damn well going to ski it!

Paul and I felt rather than skied our way down a couple of black runs (by mistake); tumbled, with great and juvenile mirth, rather than skied down a few red runs (with great rocky peaks occasionally looming out of the mist) and then retired to the most welcoming luxury of a mountain restaurant, where the rest of the world had for some hours been scoffing the most delicious Swiss cakes and pud-dings served by white-hatted chefs. For all the disappointments of the weather, Livigno seemed an awfully long way away.

When I returned on several occasions to ski St Moritz properly, I was scarcely able to recognize the area where we had first ventured. It might as well have been on Pluto. But I did manage to

Prince Charles's dream combination? Polo in the snow. It is possible to indulge in many activities in St Moritz apart from skiing.

identify one run which – had we seen the drop at the time – we would never have skied, especially as comparative novices.

Unlike so many resorts that were forged into being by the ever burgeoning ski industry, St Moritz was a flourishing winter sports resort when skiing as we know it was still in the womb. Apart from having hosted two Winter Olympics, and three Alpine Ski World Championships the resort has been the venue for no fewer than twenty-eight World Bobsleigh Championships.

Even today one could (and many do) spend weeks there without giving skiing a thought. However this would be a shame since there is so much good skiing to be enjoyed there. There are half a dozen or so distinct ski areas, totalling more than 402 kilometres (250 miles) of prepared runs: Corviglia, Corvatsch, Furtschellas, Diavolezza, Lagalb, Alp Languard and other bits and pieces. Everything is so spread out that it really helps to have a car, although there is an adequate interlinking bus service.

Many people find the best skiing area is Corvatch, but for me – and others – the 'pistes de resistances' are at Lagalb and Diavolezza, both in the ski area around the picturesque village of Pontresina whose old houses feature murals depicting scenes from country life.

Lagalb, near the Bernina Pass, has one of the most magnificent, testing and tiring black runs in Europe. Even my substantial calves felt like jelly after two or three consecutive descents. (Ten descents is supposed to be equal to skiing down Everest!)

Diavolezza (2978 metres; 9,770 feet) is one of the most stunningly beautiful glaciers in Europe, and anyone who skis in St Moritz without seeing it, or sees Diavolezza without skiing it is being deprived of a magical experience. The run from the top culminates in a breathtaking descent to Morteratsch.

Corviglia, where my friend and I skied in a white-out, is the area immediately above the main town (St Moritz Dorf). Because it is so close, sunny and facing south, and the skiing is relaxed, this is the area that most people will make for on the first day of their holiday. Some – who have fewer ambitions – may tend to remain there.

It is also the location for possibly the most celebrated and most expensive mountain res- taurant in Europe, La Marmite. Specialities include truffles and caviar. Once trapped inside, you may find it difficult to emerge before dusk. You might as well at this stage forget about skiing. Indeed, many customers do not even bother to bring their skis with them.

Corviglia is fun for two or three days, but gradually skiers tend to start moving elsewhere for a change and a challenge. And St Moritz has some of the most magnificent 'elsewheres' in Europe.

The winter of 1989/90 marks a number of anniversaries in this famous resort. Among them: one hundred and twenty-five years of winter tourism, and one hundred years of bobsleigh racing. Doubtless the champagne will be flowing. But then it always is. After all, it *is* St Moritz.

SKI FACTS

RESORT HEIGHT	1800 m
RANGE	1800 – 3303 m
BLACK RUNS	16
RED RUNS	46
BLUE RUNS	18
TOTAL	80
PISTES	400 km
LIFTS	59
LONGEST RUN	8 km

St Moritz

TOP OF THE WORLD

VERBIER

Verbier aficionados like to think that their resort is the most important thing between Mont Blanc and the Matterhorn. They call it '*Le Must des Vacances.*' They could be right. But there is a strong case in some people's minds for the concept of not one Verbier but two . . . one faintly irritating, the other visually and physically stunning.

The irritating image actually keeps quite a few people away from the resort, which is regrettable since those who do boycott the place are missing some of the most exciting skiing in Europe. What causes the irritation in their minds is an extremis of Hooray-Henryitis. This can be so disenchanting that even the average Henry or Henrietta – themselves subject to the odd innocent bout of hoorayism – can be upset by it. One Sloane of my acquaintance – a charming lady and an excellent skier – says: 'I hate Verbier! Such awful people go there!'

Awful is not the word I would use. But I know what she means. Verbier does seem to attract more than its share of people who are not only young and noisy (which ski resort does not?) but also a touch loutish and arrogant, which is really where the irritation creeps in.

Be that as it may, it seems to me a small premium to pay for such vast, spectacular and occasionally somewhat terrifying skiing – 320 kilometres (200 miles) of runs served by more than eighty-five lifts. Certainly a lot of Americans, Australians and even South Americans think it worth making the long journey to experience its exciting skiing.

Verbier is one of Switzerland's few purpose-built resorts. It started in 1950 in a small way, and what really transformed the skiing here from good to overpowering was the opening up in the early eighties of the awe-inspiring Mont Fort glacier summer skiing area, which dominates the skiing at very nearly 3352 metres (11,000 feet). The idea for

Mont Fort – a breathtaking and sometimes very difficult descent.

this dramatic expansion was already being discussed in the sixties. It envisaged a so-called 'white arena,' linking Verbier (1524 metres; 5,000 feet) with Mont Fort, Tortin and Les Attelas.

The final (for now) jewel in Verbier's crown is the colourful new cable car, which came into service as a second route up to Mont Fort at the beginning of 1988. Nicknamed 'Le Jumbo' it is the largest in Europe and takes up to 150 skiers. (During tests, it is claimed, the equivalent in weight of more than a thousand people was whisked up the mountain – a comforting thought.)

Some of the best, most exciting and difficult skiing is from Mont Gelé – perched at more than 2743 metres (9,000 feet) just below Mont Fort – down to Verbier or Tortin. Mont Fort has a breathtaking and sometimes very difficult descent under the cable car on the right of the mountain as you descend. From a distance this very black and usually bump-packed run looks almost vertical. In good conditions it is possible to ski an astonishing 3048 verticle metres (10,000 feet) from Mont Fort right down to Le Chable in the valley below.

With so much tough and even ferocious skiing, it is perhaps important to recall in resorts such as Verbier that there are areas where much gentler skiing is possible. The runs down through the trees from Savoleyres to La Tzoumaz, for example, provide a welcome contrast to the more energetic skiing higher up.

In fact they can be invaluable as well as aesthetically pleasing descents. When the tough runs of Mont Fort and Mont Gele are closed because of avalanche danger, quieter places like La Tzoumaz come into their own as crowds of slope-hungry skiers search for alternatives.

But there is plenty of other skiing to enjoy in Verbier itself even when the craggy heights are temporarily closed to mortals. After all, Verbier had some good skiing before Mont Fort and Mont Gelé were opened up. And it is, of course, still there. There is a positive cat's-cradle of lifts around Attelas, Ruinettes and the sunny, open bowl of Lac des Vaux.

Verbier, linked with nine other villages (including Haute Nendaz, where I learned to ski) and Veysonnaz now rejoices in the concept of being the 'gateway to the four valleys' – anything to try to upstage the French. The town has now sprawled all over the sunny plateau which it once occupied as a small village. It is wall-to-wall chalet country, and epitomizes the concept of chalet parties – which neatly refers both to groups of skiers in chalets and the manner in which they enjoy their evenings after a day on the slopes.

Verbier is also the end (or the beginning, depending on which way you ski it) of the famous Haute Route, a high traverse across the Alps reaching Zermatt and finally Saas Fee. For your expedition you will need special boots (which I failed to appreciate and ended up with ferocious blisters during my brief foray) and touring skis with bindings that release your heels, allowing you to 'walk' and can be snapped back into place for ordinary skiing.

Touring skis were originally fitted with seal skins to stop you sliding backwards during the relentless trudge up the mountain. The 'skins' are now made of a man-made fibre substitute. The ratio of climbing up to skiing down is something like eight to one in my experience, so you have to be keen on climbing otherwise the precious descent – dramatic

deteriorated so much that for the time being it would be dangerous to continue.

Fanatics claim that it brings out the best spirit of camaraderie and strips people of their stuffiness and inhibitions. Certainly during my two or three days on tour one man – a pinstripe-suited business-man – was in tears one day because it was all too much for him. He persevered, loved it, and became a 'changed man' with 'new values.'

There is certainly something magical and almost mystical about ski touring, especially setting off in the crisp snow amid stunning scenery during the freezing dawn. But it is hard work, and to my shame I have to admit that I would prefer to take a helicopter!

But whatever the means of transport, I would not be broken hearted to find some way to leave behind me for a day or so the braying element of the Sloane Square of the Alps – no matter how wonderful the local skiing.

and terrifying as it often is – is over too soon. You travel with two very experienced mountain guides carrying huge rucksack loads of food and equipment (my tour was led by the legendary Martin Epp). You rarely come down from the high mountains until the end of the tour, sleeping in remote but cosy mountain huts. Your guide is always up before dawn, sniffing the breeze and looking at snow conditions before deciding whether to continue. Sometimes entire days are spent waiting in the cabin because conditions have

Wall-to-wall chalets.

SKI FACTS

RESORT HEIGHT	1500 m
RANGE	1820 – 3330 m
BLACK RUNS	12
RED RUNS	40
BLUE RUNS	25
TOTAL	77
PISTES	320 km (including linked resorts)
LIFTS	84 (including linked resorts)
LONGEST RUN	10 km

VERBIER
VAL DE BAGNES

ZERMATT

On a clear winter's day, the Matterhorn – that enormous, jutting monolith of granite, whose shape is famous throughout the world – pierces the blue sky with such power that one can only gaze and gasp.

It dominates Zermatt in a way that almost no other mountain dominates any village. Indeed, short of this stunning pyramid – The Lion of Zermatt – being blasted from the sky by missiles, the Matterhorn will always guarantee that Zermatt and even Switzerland is in the very forefront of spectacular winter resorts.

It is perhaps fortunate that Zermatt's reputation depends on its tremendous natural resources (twenty-nine of Switzerland's 4000 metres-plus (over 13,000 feet) mountains jostle spectacularly almost shoulder-to-shoulder round the resort) rather than the way in which its leaders have made use of them.

There has been considerable acrimony within the now somewhat overgrown and overcrowded mountain village about whether it should be milked like a fat Swiss cow for all it is worth, or cherished more gently with at least half an eye on conservation.

Today Zermatt at 1620 metres (5,315 feet), the most southerly ski resort in Switzerland, with the highest timber line in Europe (around 2500 metres; 8,200 feet) oozes charm, opulence, extravagance, beauty and more than a hint of snobbery. But long ago, as its name suggests, it was a simple meadow with a few humble chalets where the only income was from agriculture, slightly enhanced in time with a little mountain guiding.

Gradually, as the nineteenth century unfolded, the once quaint hamlet – with its stunning chain of mountains such as Monte Rosa, Breithorn, Lyskamm, Castor and Pollux – became more and more sought-after, finally developing into one of Europe's original 'Fat Cat' resorts.

Zermatt's first winter visitors in any numbers started coming in 1927. The railway up to Riffelberg started a year later. From today's brochures, one would never suspect that all was not perfect. In the 'traffic-free' village, we are told, there remains 'just the clip-clop of the horse-drawn sleigh taxis and the gentle whirr of the electric trolleys which carry goods around.' We learn also that 'development has been carefully controlled ... The natural charm of Zermatt has not been affected.'

Sadly, not everyone would agree. The whirr of the trolleys may be gentle, but they have been known to knock tourists over almost as effectively as petrol-driven vehicles. More importantly, Zermatt's 'natural charm' is not quite what it used to be. But where do you draw the line? To ease the problems of queuing – especially during the high season – more lifts are built. This attracts more skiers. So more hotels must be considered. This leads to more queues. Oversimplified it may be, but this is Catch 22, Swiss-style.

Continuing briefly on the negative side, the ski school at Zermatt has come in for considerable criticism from the Consumer Association's *Good Skiing Guide*, which claims that classes can be too large and instructors can be unhelpful, and on some occasions do not even turn up for lessons. The guide awards the school 'a particularly black mark' and says reports about the school have been 'unfavourable.' The tourist office says these reports are out of date and claims that the ski school has pulled its socks up. Let us hope so.

Fortunately Zermatt is such a sumptuous part of the world that it would be almost impossible to spoil it completely. It has abundant restaurants (reputedly more than any other ski resort in the entire Alps), discothèques and bars.

It would perhaps be churlish to mention just one but, since I have no ice-axe to grind, I was much taken with Elsie's Bar (just by the front of the church where as a small boy I used to feed dandelion leaves to the marmots which were then kept there). Expensive, yes, but full of atmosphere, and good food (especially the oysters and snails) and company. On the mountain itself,

A closer view of the 'Lion of Zermatt', this time heading for the Theodulpass and Testa Grigia.

Enzo's Hitta in the tiny hamlet of Findeln is most highly recommended.

In 1979 Zermatt opened the highest and probably most spectacular cable-car ride in Europe – more than 3810 metres (12,500 feet) up to the Kleine Matterhorn, a dramatic, breathtaking journey. It took 25,000 helicopter flights to deposit the nine million kilos of equipment on the construction site. Those intimidated by sudden, yawning drops through mist-shrouded and craggy rock faces and ice falls should keep their eyes shut during the ascent.

While writing this I have just screened a video I shot there when the lift first opened. Not that I needed reminding – but it was heart stopping just watching it on a small screen, never mind the real thing! From the top, there is a dramatic view of the Breithorn and the huge cliff of snow that rests cream-cake-like on its summit.

As a boy I used to marvel at the Breithorn and its breathtaking companions from the Gornergrat above the spectacular icy chasm, the Gorner-gletscher. I would gaze across, spellbound. The silence was so loud and the vista so vast that it was almost deafening. In those heady days, it seemed to me to be the domain of the gods. Somehow, being able to ride up to such sacred places by cable car seems almost sacrilegious.

Having come to terms with this, however, it is intriguing to be able to ski on down into Italy and enjoy a bowl of pasta in the Cervinia sunshine. Once better known as Breuil (until Mussolini flattened it and built a ski resort there) this is the so-called 'wrong side' of the Matterhorn. It was from here, in the fateful year of 1865, that a team of Italian mountaineers set out to climb the much-feared mountain, unaware that an expedition led by the famous English mountaineer Edward Whymper had already set out from the other side.

Although victorious, four of Whymper's party were killed during the descent when the young and inexperienced Douglas Hadow slipped, knocking over one of the guides and dragged the Reverend Charles Hudson and Lord Francis Douglas off the mountain. The hemp rope broke, and the four men

The magnificent Matterhorn, guardian of the Zermatt Valley.

plunged to their doom down the 1200-metre (4,000-foot) north wall. To this day, one body – that of Lord Francis Douglas, eighteen years old when he died – has never been recovered.

The rope, plus boots and various items of clothing from the triumphant but ill-fated expedition can be seen in Zermatt's excellent museum. Although tragic, this famous climb put Zermatt on the map, and was one reason why it became such a successful winter sports resort.

The fourteen square miles of skiing (described by the tourist office as a 'snow beach for ski freaks') is divided into three main areas, and the permuta-

tions are almost endless. It makes good sense to remain in one area at a time rather than waste valuable time trying to move from one area to another on the same day.

The Gornergrat – scene of my magical childhood gazings – and Stockhorn areas bask in the sunshine for much of the day. In recent years snowmaking equipment has been installed in the Findeln, Sunegga and Unterrothorn areas and from Trockener Steg to Furri. This has already

Zermatt – its great natural beauty acts like a magnet to developers.

paid off, especially during the disastrous starts to recent winters.

There is a slow but satisfying Swiss mountain railway all the way up to Gornergrat (when inaugurated in 1898, it was the first electric rack-and-pinion railway in Switzerland). It first operated in winter for military purposes during the Second World War, and by 1948 it was running all the year round. You can also use the modern Sunegga underground railway which, in 1980, replaced the delightful but totally obsolete canvas-topped sideways-on chair lift. In three minutes, this takes you to the Blauherd-Rothorn area, from where you can reach the Gornergrat and its wonderful panorama.

The skiing around the Gornergrat and Stockhorn at 3400 metres (11,170 feet) and across to the Kleine Matterhorn area is sunny and good. The slopes above the Findeln Glacier – when they finally open in February – are among the toughest and most exciting in the Alps.

Triftji, an exhilarating and extremely tough run from the top of the Stockhorn cable car is a huge favourite with toughened mogul skiers, and distinctly alarming to gentler souls. If you are lucky, you might catch it with a blanket of precious powder. Other good blacks include National, Chamois and Marmotte. But be careful not to be carried away and ski recklessly. Zermatt recently introduced plain-clothes 'piste-police' who have the power to take away your lift pass should you be considered a dangerous skier.

Not far below the base of the Matterhorn itself – a dramatic location indeed – is the Schwarzsee area where some of Zermatt's other challenging and difficult runs, such as Aroleid and Tiefbach are situated.

In between Schwarzsee and the Kleine Matterhorn area is the Trockener-Steg area, from which you can reach the Theodulpass and Testa Grigia at 3477 metres (11,410 feet).

In summer, the pass was the traditional route used by Italian émigrés in search of jobs in kitchens (no shortage of kitchens in Zermatt!) and on roads across the Swiss border. Now it is Zermatt's summer skiing area, claimed to be the largest in Europe, with wide-open, chilly but enjoyable glacier skiing, and the point of departure – should you wish – to ski down into Cervinia. The run back to Zermatt – when it is open – is a most enjoyable thirteen kilometres (eight miles).

Up there, one cannot even hear a whisper of the altercations concerning Zermatt's future. This is for the burghers in their luxurious hotels down in the valley to worry about. We are here to ski in the shadow of the magnificent – but, it must be said, sometimes moody and mean – Matterhorn.

A handful of supermen such as Jean Marc Boivin have actually skied down it. Not all have survived. For the recreational skier, the Matterhorn is best marvelled at while skiing at a safe distance.

You cannot fail to enjoy skiing in Zermatt, with its 150 kilometres (93 miles) of prepared pistes and endless off-piste, plus the multitude of mountain restaurants for which it is also famous (sixty-five at the last count).

And no matter how many times you see photographs of the magnificent Matterhorn, none of them will prepare you for the hypnotic splendour of the real thing.

SKI FACTS

RESORT HEIGHT	1620 m
RANGE	1620 – 3820 m
BLACK RUNS	12
RED RUNS	17
BLUE RUNS	11
TOTAL	40
PISTES	150 km
LIFTS	36
LONGEST RUN	14 km

ZERMATT

ALTA

A is for Alta, but those who cherish this long-established American resort would also rate it as Alpha ... the brightest star of the world's constellation of ski resorts. It has been described as 'The Cadillac of skiing.' Indeed, according to the *American Holiday* magazine: 'Alta has one simple claim to fame ... the world's best skiing'.

When Brigham Young led his Mormon followers in the Church of the Latter-Day Saints across the plains of the Western United States and away from persecution in the Midwest in the late 1800s, he

pilgrimage to the Wasatch. They are all convinced that Young did indeed find paradise. But today these visitors might well be branded as pagans and worshippers of false gods. They have a different religion which like Young's has also spread around the world – skiing. And to Alta's most stalwart devotees, this is a cathedral of latter-day powder skiers. For them, these slopes are like shrines.

The benediction hymn here – perhaps over a whiskey and rye – might be: 'Make it deep, make it light – and keep it coming through the night.' And, to end perhaps: 'Praise ye the powder gods.' Such supplications seem to work. The snow falls from the heavens on to Alta with a munificence un-equalled almost anywhere else on earth. It is just about the best in America. And the deepest.

Like so many of America's best resorts, Alta rose from the ashes of an earlier mining industry. Soon after the Mormon pioneers arrived, silver had been discovered. Rich ore from the Michigan Mine in Grizzly Gulch (just east of Alta's present-day fire station) was transported by tramway seven miles down the main canyon. A railroad, initially mule-powered, carried refined ore to smelters in Salt Lake Valley. During the mining days, long, heavy skis or snowshoes were worn by those forced to hike along the canyon. It was, however, too much work getting back up the mountain again to ski for pleasure.

Exceptionally heavy snowfalls sometimes caused havoc with mining operations. In the 1920s a huge snowslide came churning down the mountainside and wiped out the entire village. Some saw it as a symbol of the end of the mining era and the small beginnings of the skiing age.

Although the rich silver veins were beginning to die out the mine owners noticed that every weekend people were flocking to the area from nearby Salt Lake City to hike doggedly up the mountains and then come hurtling down again on skis.

was searching for a latter-day version of the Promised Land. The arduous journey ended when he reached the Wasatch Mountains and gazed down at the Salt Lake Valley.

Now each year thousands of people from around the world follow in Young's footsteps by making a

The greatest snow on earth!

On 30th January 1938 there was no further need to walk up. Alta's first chair lift creaked its way to the top of Collins Gulch. It had been built by a group of businessmen, who formed the Salt Lake City Winter Sports Association – later to become the Alta Ski Lifts Company.

News of this rush for 'frozen gold' quickly spread around Utah. A new industry, making use of a commodity that turned out to be second to none – Utah snow – was about to burst upon the scene like an avalanche.

Now, during the ski season, more than two hundred flights a day arrive at Salt Lake's International Airport, known locally as the 'skiport.' No other American city is so close to so many ski resorts – seven altogether. You can be skiing in most of them within forty-five minutes of your arrival. The Utah tourist office likes to describe this splendid lack of time-wasting as Utah's 'eight-day ski week.'

In its day, Alta was almost certainly the finest resort for powder snow in the world. Some would say it still is. Many Americans say that this was where powder skiing was invented.

Neighbouring Snowbird – now much bigger and more famous than its elderly neighbour five minutes up the road – had not even been thought of when skiers first tasted the delights of the biggest annual 'dump' of famous fluffy Utah powder in 1937. Nor had Park City. Yet nowadays many people ski Snowbird without bothering with Alta, a mere two miles away. They might have read somewhere that Alta has a vertical drop of only 2,000 feet. And that it only has eleven lifts. Little do they know the treasures that they are missing.

Alta once stood alone, with its astonishing snow record (now shared with Snowbird) as the original focal point for powder skiing.

'Alta, the Grande Dame of Utah skiing' says an American writer, Peter Oliver, 'can squeeze snow from the most innocuous clouds as no other area can.' As a result, skiers here are sometimes warned: 'Keep your mouth shut!' A deep breath can take the light, dry powder straight into the lungs.

One of the joys of Alta is that it has hardly changed, and with luck, will not do so in the foreseeable future. Conservation is a strong force here: further building is banned, and in theory the resort is not allowed to add to its present eight

Alta has hardly changed in fifty years.

chairs and three tows. The danger of avalanches also contributes to this control – they are sufficiently regular to be a threat to any new buildings. The quality of the skiing is also an important factor. The resort manager, Chic Morton, says:

> We do not believe that we should make the capacity of our lifts greater than the runs can take and still be able to provide a good skiing experience for each guest. We are firmly convinced that skiers would rather spend a short time in lift lines rather than have to look over their shoulders all the way down an overcrowded slope.

It is not uncommon for the road from Little Cottonwood Canyon to be closed by a heavy snowfall, and sometimes when you wake up to a sunny day after a night of heavy snow, the normally hushed resort sounds more like a war-zone as helicopters whirr in all directions, cannons explode and hand-grenades pop as the road and slopes are cleared for incoming skiers.

I skied Alta on the way back from an 'Interconnect' tour from Snowbird, taking in the resorts of Solitude and Brighton (see page 155).

The Interconnect was once known only to 'mountain men, wildlife and a small corps of tight-lipped powder hounds . . .' But now anyone with a taste for adventure and a reasonable off-piste technique can join in. I found Alta's Baldy Chutes – with their narrow, breathtaking drops – a delight. And I particularly enjoyed the High Rustler trail – long, steep and mogully, or chest-deep in dry powder. Among the other tougher runs are Nina Curve, Schuss Gully and Collins Face. And the Germania lift services other expert trails such as Race Course, Sun Spot, Yellow Trail and Lone Pine. Spiny Ridge has a number of excellent long chutes such as Sidewinder and Glory Hole, which has a most appropriately named 'cut-off': Angina Chute.

There is no guide service to help the unfamiliar find their way through the maze of trails in Alta and the locals like to keep it that way. So secret powder spots of Wildcat, Supreme, Westward Ho, Eagle's Nest or the Greeley Bowls are like a cache of silver which they can horde for themselves. Other excellent skiing can be found on the left of the

Wildcat below Devil's Castle. There is also an exciting 'hump-back' ridge between Wildcat and Albion Basin. The Albion lift – originally called Never Sweat – serves the Crooked Mile, an undulating run that provides an almost perfect 'ego' descent for beginners. Some of the best skiing can only be reached by taking your skis off and walking up. Like other religions, powder skiing can involve making sacrifices. With so much exciting skiing, it comes as a surprise to discover that Alta offers one of the best lift-ticket rates in the US.

There are those who believe that Alta is one of the great secrets of the USA. I tend to agree. On a good day after a fresh fall of powder, it is certainly difficult to imagine a more satisfying and inspiring ski area. And I can understand why Alta's most dedicated enthusiasts describe its skiing as something close to a religious experience.

SKI FACTS

TRAILS	35
EASIEST	25%
MORE DIFFICULT	40%
MOST DIFFICULT	35%
PEAK ELEVATION	10,550 ft
VERTICAL DROP	2,000 ft
LONGEST RUN	3½ miles
CHAIR LIFTS	8 doubles
TOWS	3
AVERAGE SNOWFALL	550 in

ASPEN

spen, Colorado. Those words probably say more about skiing to the public at large than any other two words in the English language. 'When it comes to skiing' a friend of mine from Los Angeles said to me recently, 'this is kind'a IT!' Actually, he was discussing heli-skiing in the Canadian Rockies, but many Americans reckon Aspen *is* kind'a it. Indeed, there is a sign just outside the resort which trumpets: 'There's Only One!'

But why?

The main reason is that a kind of mystique has enveloped the town over the years. An uncontrollable mystique that is not altogether justified by fact. But then perhaps mystique rarely is.

Aspen, once known as the Crystal City of the Rockies, has been described as a combination of Beverly Hills and the true spirit of the Old West. There is no denying that Aspen Mountain, or Ajax Mountain as the locals know it (it has yet a third name – the Bell) has that certain pedigree that is instantly recognizable. For want of a better word, Aspen has 'class'. But then class is not what everyone wants, and there are those who have abandoned Aspen for other American resorts which are more basic, less pretentious, just as exciting and perhaps more real.

Jackson Hole, Wyoming, for example, is like a breath of fresh if sometimes rather cold air by comparison. So too are resorts like Telluride, Taos and Breckenridge.

Much as I love Aspen and its skiing, which is undeniably first class, there is something slightly phoney about the place. However, perhaps that is true of all the great skiing showplaces the world over where people go to be seen – but not necessarily on the slopes. It is true of St Moritz. It is true of Courchevel. And it is true of Cortina.

Aspen, like many American ski resorts, was originally an old mining town. Most of the early miners who were brave enough to venture across the fearsome Independence Pass from Leadville on their Norwegian-style snowshoes in 1870 were beaten back not by the weather but by the Ute Indians. But eventually the Ute chief, Ouray, calmed the situation, and the miners streamed back over the pass again into what became known as Roaring Fork Valley. This was the beginning of Aspen, originally christened Ute City. In the 1880s the miners discovered one of the richest silver mines in the world. During the boom, Aspen's population grew to twelve thousand and they built two railroads, three banks, three schools, six newspapers, a hospital, an opera house, ten churches and of course a flourishing brothel area.

By the turn of the century, children from the town had started to enjoy a primitive form of skiing. They would strap boards to their feet and slide straight down the mountain. Turning was a refinement with which they had yet to concern themselves. Little could they have known that one day their strange hobby would prove to be far more important than the present life-blood of the community, silver.

For Aspen – just like all the other mining towns – there were troubled times ahead. With the end of the silver standard in 1893 most mines closed and the local economy became dependant on ranchers and potato farmers. By the 1930s the population had dwindled to four hundred.

It was not long after this that a small group of investors hired a Swiss avalanche expert, André Roche, to survey the area and attempt to find the best location for a ski resort. The Second World War intervened. But Roche formed the Roaring Fork Winter Sports Club, which was eventually renamed the Aspen Ski Club.

Skiing had come to stay.

Aspen – 'this is kind'a it'!

The first trail was called Roche Run. And the first lift was built – two sledges, each carrying ten people pulled up the hill by snow track with two mine hoists and a gas motor. By 1941, the National Downhill and Slalom races were being held at Aspen. And when America joined in the war, the US Army's 10th Mountain Division started training at Aspen (and Vail).

Immediately after the war, the Aspen Ski Company was formed by Friedl Pfeifer, one of those 10th Mountain Division troops and a Chicago industrialist, Walter Paepcke (pronouncing the names of this partnership – Pfeifer and Paepcke – proved more difficult than some of the skiing).

By 1947, the first proper lifts were opening. Aspen had become a real ski resort.

Celebrities began to home in on the town, and it quickly became the most fashionable ski area in the States. Apart from being fashionable, it so happens that the skiing there is rather spectacular.

Aspen Mountain has a reputation for being tough, with no skiing terrain at all for beginners, which is very unusual. However, it is not altogether true. There *are* runs that beginners could cope with. The reason that they are not encouraged to ski on the mountain is that although the area looks (and is) beautifully laid out, it has one major snag. There is a serious bottleneck near the bottom. So at the end of the day there would be a risk of faltering, unsteady beginners being battered to one side like slalom poles by fast skiers scorching down Copper Bowl or Ruthie's Run like Exocets. If only there were an easy alternative route off the mountain, more timid skiers would be able to enjoy some of the gentler skiing higher up. They can get to it easily enough now that the Silver Queen Gondola has been installed. It is getting down again that poses the problem.

Perhaps one has to accept, reluctantly, that Aspen Mountain is best left to strong intermediates and experts.

The expert-only runs will test your courage and your skill.

Opposite
Bump enthusiasts on the mogul trail.

It is a pretty mountain, with pines, spruces and firs lining many of the trails (as Americans call pistes). Trees grow at a much higher altitude in the American mountains than they do in Europe, so it is much rarer to find yourself above the tree-line – often such a bleak prospect in Europe.

If Capability Brown had planned ski resorts as well as gardens, he would have been proud to have his name linked with Aspen Mountain. It is beautifully designed, rather like an elegant adventure playground. The really rough, tough, so-called 'double-black diamond' runs peel off like Red Arrow smoke-trails at the edges of the main skiing area. There are five in a row running parallel off the International trail: Bear Paw, Zaugg Dump, Perry's Prowl, Last Dollar and Short Snort (an unintentional reminder that some Aspenites were until quite recently renowned for being rather free and easy with drugs).

They look innocent enough as you begin, but the double-diamond signs relay a message to your brain rather reminiscent of a skull-and-cross-bones. You know that round the corner or over the next few bumps the trail, like Beachy Head, will fall away alarmingly leaving you with little choice but to ski a mogulled precipice that will seriously test your skill and nerve. But these 'expert-only' runs are easily avoided. Indeed, you have to go slightly out of your way to find them – rather like turning off a motorway when you are having perfectly good fun zooming along without any need for extra excitement. But they are always there, lurking to the right of you as you ski International and North Star, should you want them.

The ride to Sundeck at the top of the mountain (11,200 feet) takes just thirteen minutes by the Silver Queen. The gondola takes six skiers and is claimed to be the biggest single-stage gondola in the world. The longest run is three miles – from One and Two Leaf via North Star and Gentleman's Ridge to Little Nell.

Aspen amuses the rich and famous both on and off the piste.

There are seventy-five trails covering 625 acres, with some good skiing in the back bowls which you can experience through powder tours by snow-cat. This is a piste-grooming machine converted to transport skiers to good off-piste slopes.

Aspen claims over 1,400 acres of back-country terrain to explore, with tree-shaded glades and open, sunlit bowls. For your $150 or so, they throw in a big picnic lunch and enchanting views of the Elk Mountains. Each tour averages around eight runs of one thousand verticle feet. It is almost as good as helicopter skiing – without the same degree of excitement.

Aspen town itself is probably the most sophisticated, glitzy, and trendy ski resort in North America. It is also the haunt, as one colour magazine writer has put it, of the 'mega-filthy-rich' who like to pretend that Aspen is just like any other ski resort . . . a sort of inverse snobbery. Something like thirty millionaires own property there – and no doubt that is a conservative estimate. Some women actually *ski* in fur jackets, let alone parade around town in them. A number of film stars like Clint Eastwood, have set up home in the surrounding foothills. Jack Nicholson has *two* homes here. Those who do not actually live here would rarely wish to be seen anywhere else. The list of VIP visitors is endless . . . Charlton Heston, John Denver, Michael Douglas, Robert Wagner, Martina Navratilova, Chris Lloyd and many others.

Where there are 'stars', of course, there is usually the occasional scandal. Aspen's most famous such episode involved the shooting of a ski instructor, Spider Sabich, by Claudine Longet, the former wife of Andy Williams. But this unhappy incident apart, Aspen's rich and famous appear to lead fairly blameless if indulgent existences.

One of the many attractions of Aspen is that you can fly almost straight on to the ski slopes. Apart from regular scheduled flights from Denver, the principal airport serving Colorado, there are now direct flights from Chicago, Dallas, Los Angeles, Long Beach and San Francisco.

The town, twinkling with Victorian street lamps and all-winter-round Christmas-style lights boasts scores of restaurants scattered around its cobbled sidewalks and pedestrian malls. Several have twenties- or thirties-style decor, with a fair scattering of art deco fittings. There is also a wide selection of snazzy hotels, including the famous and recently revamped Jerome Hotel which has just enjoyed its one hundredth birthday.

Both the Jerome and the Wheeler Opera House were built by Jerome Wheeler, then president of Macy's department store in New York City. Miners used to celebrate their silver strikes in the Jerome Bar. Now skiers celebrate a day's glorious powder skiing there. The hotel claims that 'if you haven't been to the Jerome Bar, you haven't been to Aspen.'

My feeling is that if you have not skied Aspen, you have not skied Colorado.

SKI FACTS

TRAILS	75 (23 miles in 625 acres)
EASIEST	0%
MORE DIFFICULT	35%
MOST DIFFICULT	35%
EXPERT	30%
PEAK ELEVATION	11,212 ft
VERTICAL DROP	3,267 ft
LONGEST RUN	3 miles
GONDOLAS	6-passenger Silver Queen
CHAIR LIFTS	7 (3 quads and 4 doubles)
AVERAGE SNOWFALL	300 in

BRECKENRIDGE

The golden rule in powder – shut your mouth!

For a place once officially listed as a ghost town (population: 7) and worse still, not even acknowledged to be part of America until a mere fifty odd years ago, the former mining town of Breckenridge is enjoying a wonderful resurrection.

Times have changed since Tom Groves made the place famous when he discovered the largest single gold nugget ever found in Colorado. It was named 'Tom's Baby,' and weighed in at thirteen stone five pounds. The year was 1887.

A century later, in 1987, Breckenridge was celebrating another kind of achievement altogether. For the fourth consecutive year, the number of skiers visiting the resort had broken all records,

and it claimed to be enjoying the highest growth rate of any ski resort in America. The trend continues today. In 1987/88, for the first time, the resort celebrated a million 'skier days'.

Both the skiing *and* the skiers reach great heights here. Peak 8 (Breckenridge does not waste words on its mountains – it just gives them numbers) has skiing up to 12,213 feet. (Its smaller neighbour, Copper Mountain, rather to Breckenridge's irritation, can top that by 147 feet.)

Breckenridge, part of the region's 'Ski The Summit' area (with Keystone, Copper Mountain, and Arapahoe Basin) has three main mountains: Peak 8, where the ski resort really started and which has 888 acres of skiing (more than the other two peaks combined); Peak 9; and the latest, opened in 1985. This, it may come as little surprise to learn, was christened Peak 10.

Peak 10 is pretty tough (sixty-seven per cent advanced, thirty-one per cent intermediate and only two per cent beginner). Peak 9 is gentler, with long, cruising skiing (eleven per cent advanced, forty-six per cent intermediate and forty-three per cent beginner). Peak 8 is more mixed, but the emphasis is definitely towards the more difficult (sixty-three per cent advanced, twenty-one per cent intermediate and sixteen per cent beginner). Just to make matters confusing, one of the most challenging runs (Shock) is on the 'easy' mountain (Peak 9) and one of the easiest (Flapjack) is on the most difficult (Peak 10).

Breckenridge, which started life as a mining camp when gold was discovered along the banks of Blue River in 1859, is now enjoying skiing success of near gold-rush proportions, attracting well over 100,000 each season. It is not difficult to see why.

The resort is proud of its policy of ploughing a considerable proportion of its profits back into the mountains as high-speed uphill transport. During recent years two high-speed 'quad' (quadruple-seated) chairs have been added to the resort. There is now one for each peak.

These 'superchairs' travel at one thousand feet a minute. One of them, Quicksilver, on Peak 9 – said to be the world's first – has been upgraded to take more than three thousand skiers an hour, which is now claimed also to be the world's fastest. On Peak 8, the Colorado Super Chair takes skiers to the summit in six-and-a-half minutes.

Almost sixty miles of good-to-excellent skiing are spread out for the Breckenridge visitor to sample, and these chairs speed up the process considerably, although the claim that they are 'as fast as a rifle bullet' is over-egging things a trifle. But because so much time in skiing resorts is spent returning to the top of the mountain and so little – in relative terms – actually skiing down it, a chair which travels faster than average is a godsend to a keen skier anxious to pack as much downhill time into his daily itinerary as possible.

Is it four planes? (No – it's super quad.)

The three mountains, which stretch across the Ten Mile Range, offer a vast amount of on-piste skiing ... 110 trails, which is more than Vail. Among them are some of the best and imaginatively named mogul runs in Colorado. Spitfire, Psychopath, Mach 1 and Goodbye Girl – a name and indeed a run that evokes near-suicide! – spring to mind. Some sections have a fall-line not dissimilar to Dover's White Cliffs. There is also snow-making machinery covering more than four hundred acres (mainly on Peak 9) and helicopter skiing if you want to indulge yourself.

Not for a moment backward in coming forward about their resort, the marketing department claim that Breckenridge has the most expert trails in Colorado. It certainly has a wild, mustang-like quality. This came as quite a surprise since the owners, until recently, were the Aspen Skiing Company. (A Japanese sports goods and ski equipment company, Victoria of Tokio bought Breckenridge in 1988.) One would never have thought that Aspen would admit that anywhere other than their own beloved resort could possibly be upstaged in any department by another. However, one has to admire their honesty. The Japanese obviously agree with them.

Great resort though Aspen is, it cannot really compete with the sheer size of Breckenridge unless you include one of its associated resorts of Buttermilk, Aspen Highlands or Snowmass.

Although the tree-line in America is much higher than in Europe, the skiing in Breckenridge is so high that four hundred acres of it, mainly on Peak 8 with runs like Forget-Me-Not and Pika, is above the trees. For the winter of 1988/89, a further forty-six acres of ski trails were cut – one new run for each peak – which brought the total skiing terrain to 1,526 acres. There are 180 ski instructors: one compulsive statistician has worked out that they have over one thousand years of cumulative experience between them.

The eight thousand people who had flocked over Hoosier Pass to Breckenridge by 1860 – just a year after the gold rush there started – could scarcely have imagined that their town would die and then rise Phoenix-like to be admired by thousands of

Breckenridge – ghost town turned ski mecca.

tourists who had come not to pan for gold but to slide down their mountain on skis.

In those early days snow was just something that got seriously in the way of fortune hunting. In the winter of 1898, for example, it snowed every single day in Breckenridge.

Because of surveying errors, Blue River Valley was never included in treaty negotiations, and thus Breckenridge was never officially part of America until 1936. These days it would certainly be difficult to 'lose' the valley. Skiing – if not mining – has made Breckenridge a household name.

Unlike Europe, where once a ski resort has opened, it almost invariably stays open, America has something of a history of 'losing' resorts. It is by no means unknown for a resort to open, succeed for a while, and then go out of business – and stay closed.

I would bet my last dollar that Breckenridge will never be in that category. It is the brightest, breeziest, most dynamic and friendliest of resorts, and typifies all that is best in America with precious little of all that is worst. It is also one of the closest major Colorado resorts to Denver airport (eighty miles). And a huge new area – Peak 7 – is planned.

A stroll down the main street, where so many of the old Victorian buildings (350 of them) have been carefully preserved or recreated, is a genuine pleasure and evokes a strong feeling of gold-rush days – although the present-day well-to-do ambiance is probably not a very accurate representation of the tough, rough-and-ready days of the real mining era. But all in all – with its breathtaking skiing and quaint old town – Breckenridge is definitely made of 'The Right Stuff.'

SKI FACTS

	Peak 8	Peak 9	Peak 10	Total
TRAILS	110 (1,526 acres)			
EASIEST	16%	43%	2%	21%
MORE DIFFICULT	21%	46%	31%	32%
MOST DIFFICULT	63%	11%	67%	47%
PEAK ELEVATION	12,213 ft			
VERTICAL DROP	2,713 ft			
CHAIR LIFTS	6 (1 quad and 5 doubles)	6 (1 quad, 1 triple and 4 doubles)	1 quad	
TOWS				
AVERAGE SNOWFALL	255 in			

BRECKENRIDGE
GENUINE COLORADO

HEAVENLY VALLEY

Describing a ski resort which has seven gambling casinos waiting for you at the bottom of the mountain as 'heavenly' is perhaps a matter of interpretation. However in spite of being half in Nevada and close to some of the more sinister elements of American society, the resort's name is far from being a misnomer.

The skiing can indeed be heavenly, and the stunningly contrasting scenery is certainly 'awesome', to use a Californianism. Many skiers find that the thrill of skiing flat out robs them of the chance of enjoying the scenery. That could hardly be more appropriate than at Heavenly Valley.

The more heavenly looking side is in California, where what has been described as the world's most beautiful alpine lake, Tahoe, stretches out below you, shimmering in the sunshine.

On the Nevada side, the scenery is almost equally spectacular and totally different. Although none-the-less visually awe-inspiring, it veers more towards one's impressions of what hell might be like rather than heaven. There, also stretched out before you, is the seemingly endless, hazy, bakingly hot Nevada desert.

The perfect place to see both visions in one vast panorama is from the Sky Chair which takes you to the highest point in this High Sierras resort, Monument Peak (10,167 feet) which straddles both states. Although you may be basking in Californian sunshine, it can suddenly turn cold, with gusts of

The view of Lake Tahoe and the Nevada desert can stop you in your tracks.

resorts also claim this distinction (they tend to have different criteria for what constitutes 'largest') suffice it to say that Heavenly, like its ethereal counterpart, has room for anyone 'good' enough to want to be there!

The resort has recently been involved in some major new lift installations. The Comet, a detachable 'quad' chair on the Nevada side climbs to Little Dipper Knob, replacing the old East Peak double chair. A new triple chair and two new doubles have also been installed, and there is now snow-making equipment all the way to the Nevada summit.

Arctic wind that can make your chair swing from side to side with alarming force.

As you ski down the Skyline Trail, you hardly know which way to look – lakewards or desert-wards. The consequence of this dramatic choice of scenery is that you tend not to look where you are skiing and are therefore inclined to fall over the edge. Best to stop, drink it all in, take your pictures and then enjoy the skiing.

There is so much skiing on *both* sides of the mountain that the average skier could spend a whole week on the Californian side without even glimpsing what was on the Nevada side yet not become bored – and vice-versa. Indeed, Heavenly claims to be America's largest ski area. Since other

SKI FACTS

TRAILS	20 square miles
EASIEST	25%
MORE DIFFICULT	50%
MOST DIFFICULT	25%
PEAK ELEVATION	10,167 ft
VERTICAL DROP	2,600 ft
CHAIR LIFTS	17 (1 quad, 7 triples and 9 doubles)
TOWS	6
AVERAGE SNOWFALL	400 in

Nowadays, like many American ski resorts, Heavenly – where the sun is supposed to shine during eighty per cent of the winter months – provides ski 'hostesses' to show first-time visitors the way round the mountain. 'Heavenly Hostess' has a wonderful ring about it. Especially when her name is Bambi, as turned out to be the case during my first visit. In Heavenly even the male species are angelic. The resort describes its ski instructors as 'friendly, professional and handsome'.

As Bambi and her heavenly colleagues Vikki and Susie lure you to the vast network of trails, you quickly realize that variety, as well as scenery, is the hallmark of Heavenly Valley: special 'Mitey Mites' lifts for beginners on both sides of the resort; ego-boosting runs with flattering names for intermediates such as Von Schmidt Trail, Olympic Downhill, Bonanza Bowl, Stage Coach and Orion's Belt; and good, gutsy runs for experts such as What The Hell, Mens Downhill, Gunbarrel (where the resort's first chair was built in 1955) and Pistol. Arguably the most difficult run is the Gunbarrel mogul field, which takes you hurtling all the way to the bottom of the mountain. Twenty five per cent of the skiing is suitable for beginners, fifty per cent for intermediates and the remaining quarter is raw meat – and drink– for experts!

Heavenly provides more than twenty square miles of skiing terrain, with twenty-six lifts, including an aerial 'tram' – the American word for a cable car. It claims an average snowfall of three hundred to five hundred inches. Although the snow in the Tahoe resorts does not have the same dryness as that in Utah's Wasatch range, this puts it among America's heaviest annual falls. Snowbird, with an average of 550 inches, claims to have more snow than anywhere in America. Unlike the current situation in Switzerland and Austria where for environmental reasons skiing among the trees is now discouraged, Heavenly and many American resorts actually encourage the practice. In fact, powder skiing in the trees makes good sense in one way because since the snow there cannot be 'groomed' it might as well be left for 'powderhounds' to enjoy. Apart from its spectacular skiing, and vertical drop of 2,600 feet, Heavenly Valley's main claim to fame is its proximity to America's gambling mecca. Indeed, one of Lake Tahoe's most famous hotels, the Cal-Neva lodge, is actually divided by the state-line and therefore gambling is legal in one part of the building and illegal in the other. Gambling tables and fruit machines abound right up to the state-line, which neatly bisects the fireplace. Unimportant facilities such as the hotel lobby have been carefully exiled to the Californian side.

Such is the preoccupation with the state border that the local town is even called Stateline. This, for those who are fascinated with the Las Vegas lifestyle, serves as a scaled-down version of Nevada's most famous city. But even scaled down, the gambling areas – mostly in action for twenty-four hours – are vast.

Imagine the biggest Marks and Spencer store you have ever seen. Fill it in your mind's eye with row upon row of fruit machines, and you have some idea of what just one of the many Stateline gambling areas resembles. There are also Las Vegas-style shows, where world-famous artists such as Sinatra, Tom Jones and Sammy Davies Jr have appeared.

For those who enjoy that sort of atmosphere, Heavenly Valley offers a unique blend of superb skiing and glitzy entertainment . . . plus all kinds of 'eateries' from Polynesian and Vietnamese to 'eat-all-you-can' establishments. It could only happen in America.

As the resort's blurb-writers themselves put it: 'Just minutes away from Heavenly's slopes, a dazzling spectrum of nightlife abounds at seven world-famous casinos offering top-name entertainment on the glittering South Shore of Lake Tahoe.'

Gambling even comes at the top of the list of Heavenly Valley's 'endless winter activities' above such pursuits as snowmobiling, ice skating, riding, boat cruises, hiking, fishing, sleigh rides and swimming.

But all good things must come to an end, even though it may only be for a summer break. At most American ski resorts, day-passes have a mysterious (to you at least) code word stamped on them designed to prevent counterfeit tickets. The letters are only decided at the last possible moment.

On the last day of the season at Heavenly, my four-letter word said: TGIO. I thought about that for a while and then gave up. Eventually someone told me what it stood for: Thank God It's Over!

Even in Heavenly, it seems, bliss is rationed.

JACKSON HOLE

The Teton mountains rise like giant sharks teeth from the huge, flat plain of Jackson Hole. The effect is utterly breathtaking. And you have yet even to climb out of the aircraft.

You have just touched down at an airport with one of the most exquisite views in the world. It is something like the equivalent of flying into Srinagar airport in Kashmir and finding you have landed next to Nanga Parbat, one of the mightiest peaks in the Himalayas. There are no foothills to reduce the impact of the Tetons. Only the sixty-mile long valley floor, or 'hole' through the Rockies, which stretches eighteen miles across to the Gros Ventre (Fat Stomach) mountains on the horizon, and the starkly, stunningly beautiful peaks of the Grand, Upper and Middle Tetons which jut suddenly skywards. With their snow-encrusted peaks shimmering in the powerful Wyoming sun, they form with Mounts Owen, Teewinot, and Nez Perce Peak what is known as the Cathedral Group.

It is indeed as mystical a spot as one could encounter in any place of worship on the planet . . . a sublime thought, made faintly ridiculous perhaps by the fact that Tetons is a French word for breasts.

Teton Village by night – a touch of Wyoming gemutlichkeit.

They were given that name by French-Canadian trappers who frequented this spectacular valley in the early nineteenth century.

The 'hole' is sealed at either end by the Salt River Range to the south and Yellowstone plateau to the north. Other holes have changed their names – Pierre's Hole, for example is now called Teton Basin, and Little Jackson's Hole has become Hoback Basin.

The name Wyoming itself is based on a word meaning 'large plateau between the mountains' – a much more romantic-sounding word than 'hole.' Wyoming is very much a mountain state: its average elevation is 6,700 feet and its highest point reaches 13,785 feet.

Although the ski resort of Jackson Hole is in the Teton range, it does not include the Cathedral Group, which is unskiable to all but the supreme expert. In fact it was not until 1971 that an unassuming, unlikely looking hero called Bill Briggs became the first man to ski the Grand Teton – 13,770 feet of fearsome, almost vertical rock.

'For all its loveliness,' said an account in *Along the Ramparts of the Tetons* by Robert B Betts, 'the Grand is a lousy mountain to ski, and its lack of chair-lifts is the least of its problems. Snow conditions vary from dreadful to sublime. If you slip, you could fall for the rest of your life.'

For thousands of years the valley and its silent Teton sentinels were hidden – 'lost' long before it

found its way to the very heart of this once-secret paradise now referred to by some as the 'last and best of the West.' Not just one service, but several. Airlines as diverse as American, Continental, Delta, Mesa, Rocky Mountain, SkyWest and United have recently opened up Jackson Hole to such a degree that one half fears that this stunning ski area could be spoilt. The average customer, according to the resort, 'travels 1,400 miles. And that's just one way!'

From the airport, it is only another twelve miles drive to the town of Jackson, a wild-west settlement with its cowboy bars – the Million Dollar Cowboy Bar even has saddles instead of bar stools. Another, The Wort Hotel's Silver Dollar Bar, has more than two thousand silver dollars inlaid in rows in the counter. The sidewalks are wooden – similar to those that gunslingers once thudded slowly along with their spurs jangling before a shoot-out.

Country-and-Western bands perform, and in the main cowboy bar, a huge stuffed grizzly stands bolt upright in a glass case looking just as ferocious as it did on the day it was shot by a trapper not far from town.

Although bears are rare around here now, it is not far to the edge of Yellowstone National Park where grizzlies roam side by side with coyote, elk, moose and buffalo in the strange world of mud-pots, hot-springs and geysers (pronounced guysers by the locals).

Moose even wander around the outskirts of Jackson, and it is not uncommon to glimpse a mother and calf by the roadside in the moonlight. And right on Jackson's doorstep is the largest elk reservation in America. (To be pedantic, they are not really elk at all, but wapiti. They were mis-named elk by the early European hunters and settlers and the mistake stuck. To make things even more complicated, what they called moose should really have been called elk.)

Sometimes, as the sun rises over Sleeping Indian – a peak in the Gros Ventre range that looks for all the world like an Indian chief lying flat on his back with full headdress – thousands of elk can be seen roaming the fields below.

was ever found. Then game began to find its way into the rich pastures. And man followed. Indians came: Snake, Crow, Blackfoot and Gros Ventre. And then the trappers and mountain men – from Canada, America, Britain and even from Spain and Germany. Among them was the legendary Butch Cassidy. It was one of these tough adventurers, Davey Jackson – for whom the valley was an especially happy hunting ground between 1807 and 1840 – who gave it his name (originally Jackson's Big Hole).

Nowadays, although it is still probably the furthest ski resort from any major population centre, travelling to this remote part of Wyoming is less daunting. The mighty passenger airliner has

Jackson – perhaps the greatest ski resort in the world with America's only 4,000-foot vertical drop.

From Jackson it is only another twelve miles to the actual ski resort, based around Teton Village (6,300 feet) at the base of the area's principal peak, Rendezvous Mountain (10,400 feet). It is a great, craggy, powder-keg of a mountain, which proudly boasts the USA's only 4,000-foot vertical drop.

Somehow, with the number of lifts scarely reaching double figures, there is an extraordinary amount of skiing. The trails are swashbuckling, breathtaking, rugged, tough, gutsy and exhilarating. The view across the valley – especially once you are up on the mountain – is staggering. You feel mesmerized by the sheer space of it all, and can only stop skiing, catch your breath and gaze in wonder when you are first confronted by such an astonishing vista.

Rendezvous Mountain was 'discovered' by Paul McCollister in the late fifties. He stumbled across it while searching for a ski mountain nearer Jackson at Cache Creek. 'I found it quite overwhelming' he said to me as we skied it together. 'I went back to look at it again and again, climbing up on skins, and studying it from the air in a helicopter.' He had chanced upon one of the wonders of the ski world.

When the resort opened in 1965, the marketing was fierce and machismo. Jackson Hole in those days was not for the squeamish. It was sold as a rough, tough, unyielding resort for crack skiers only. Later McCollister realized this had been a mistake. Beginners and timid intermediates shyed away from Jackson Hole as though it were Wyoming's famous bucking bronco.

McCollister started to promote the gentler face of Jackson Hole – Apres-Vous mountain, the Dr Jekyll to Rendezvous's Mr Hyde. Apres-Vous (actually the north shoulder of Rendezvous) has slopes which are much more user-friendly, with scenery that is just as remarkable, and the Jackson Hole magic is only slightly watered down.

But for the ambitious skier, Rendezvous has few rivals. It is riddled with rocky gulleys, steep, tree-lined chutes (couloirs), and wide-open, ungroomed descents such as the Hobacks that seem to hang in mid-air above the village way below. Many of their names are appropriate: Buffalo Bowl, Thunder, Avalanche.

Old antlers piled high in Jackson. They are shed naturally.

The most celebrated demon in Jackson's crown is Corbet's Couloir. Corbet's – named after Barry Corbet – lies at the top of the tram and is somewhat terrifying to behold. To conquer it, one must leap from an overhanging cornice, fly through the air, and land on the couloir fifteen feet below, before hurtling on down the chute which continues to be excessively steep for the next fifteen feet. 'Continuing' is more or less guaranteed. Whether you accomplish this on skis or as a tumbling human wreck is a matter of skill and a degree of luck. It is a challenge that haunts many strong skiers. At first they hurry past it to avoid being mentally sucked in like ski lemmings, but the chances are that sooner or later they will just have to jump in. Mr Corbet modestly claimed that he was not really the first to do it. He hiked up the couloir and then skied it. Another brave skier, Lonnie Ball, a ski patrolman, is credited with being the first person actually to jump into Corbet's in 1966.

But there is something much more chilling lurking a little further round the corner from Corbet's which would put blind terror into the soul of any sane man. It is called, quite undramatically, S & S. These are the initials of the surnames of two men who skied the unthinkable – a couloir that makes Corbet's look like a fun run for intermediates. It is so desperately steep and deep that only a handful of men try it each season. One, a handsome young fellow called John Griber has actually done it on a snowboard a number of times. And on one particularly insane day, he jumped it twice.

However, for mere mortals who want some excitement without necessarily risking a posthumous Gorge Medal (sic) there are plenty more chutes to be skied without having to go for quite such 'big air' (as the Americans describe being airborne on skis).

Tower Three Chute and Expert Chutes are more than enough to scare the ski pants off most skiers. Unlike so many couloirs in Europe where the tree-line is much lower, American chutes are usually tree-lined. So one cannot turn as a matter of whim. Spruce trees move quickly and do not generally take avoiding action.

As its name implies, Apres-Vous mountain is a much more docile sort of place, with gentle trails like Eagle's Rest, Pooh Bear, and Teewinot Gulley to give confidence to the debutant and more nervous skier.

The locals often say 'if you don't like the weather in the Rockies, hang on for five minutes.' The weather *can* change dramatically in Wyoming but whether you have had a ferocious, sweat-drenched adventure in a powder-blizzard on Rendezvous or a gentle cruise around Apres-Vous in bright sunshine, you are pretty certain to get a crackling, fire-side welcome after you have cruised down 'Way Home' and you are back down in the friendly atmosphere of Teton Village. Like the Tetons piercing the heavens, in my view the ski resort of Jackson Hole towers above all others.

SKI FACTS

TRAILS	81 (3,000 acres)
EASIEST	10%
MORE DIFFICULT	40%
MOST DIFFICULT	50%
PEAK ELEVATION	10,450 ft
VERTICAL DROP	4,139 ft
TRAMS	1
CHAIR LIFTS	7 (5 doubles, 1 triple and 1 quad)
TOWS	1
AVERAGE SNOWFALL	456 in

JACKSON HOLE®

KILLINGTON

Ever since Bing Crosby dreamed of a *White Christmas*, the ski resorts of New England have been able to exploit a huge market in the big cities such as New York, Washington and Boston. So says Elizabeth Hussey in Debrett's *World Of Ski*, and it is rather a nice way of putting it.

And if there is a quintessential New England resort it is Killington, the 'St Moritz of the East'

158 miles from Boston and only a five-hour drive from New York City, in the rolling Green Mountains of Vermont, the 'Green Mountain State.'

Killington has set a standard that has over the years characterized America: big. Big 'bucks', big slopes, big snow-making, longest season and longest gondola. It is the 'Jupiter' of the system of resorts east of the Mississippi that dwarfs all the other resorts. Mount Killington and its five satellite

mountains are so much larger than anything else in the US Eastern Standard Time zone that its competitors could not match it in their most optimistic fantasies. Instead, some ski areas in the east are on the defensive, claiming that they would not want to emulate their sprawling neighbour anyway.

Killington has 108 trails totalling almost eighty miles, six lodges, eighteen lifts and 721 acres of

SKI FACTS

TRAILS	108 (721 acres/ 80 miles; 66 with snow-making equipment)
EASIEST	45%
MORE DIFFICULT	20%
MOST DIFFICULT	35%
PEAK ELEVATION	4,241 ft
VERTICAL DROP	3,160 ft
GONDOLAS	Killington gondola
CHAIR LIFTS	15 (5 quads, 4 triples and 6 doubles)
TOWS	2
ANNUAL SNOWFALL	237 in

Killington VERMONT

Killington can boast the biggest ski area in the east.

skiing. There has been a huge snow-making programme recently (described as the best and most expensive in the world) which virtually guarantees skiing from October to June even when nature is at her most reticent.

To continue the Jupiter analogy for a moment, Killington's gravitational pull certainly draws resistance in some quarters. Many people – especially those with environmental and conservational zeal – prefer the concept that 'small is beautiful' and tend to regard Killington as an oversized out-of-control giant. It is not difficult to understand such sentiments. No other state in the US places such emphasis on quality rather than quantity. Strict development laws, combined with anti-litter enforcement and a ban on billboards have by and large prevented the sloppy, fast-food look that seems to pervade so much of the landscape in parts of America.

Killington is undeniably robust, but this has not been achieved without a degree of that other American weakness – overkill. The ethos behind much of its growth is somewhat similar to the so-called pressure/volume equation used in chemistry. In other words: the number of people in Manhattan divided by the fastest lifts and as many trails as possible = as huge and profitable a mountain as possible.

Preston Leete Smith, the man behind that equation, did not spend years in the laboratory or on a computer refining such a concept. He simply hiked into the woods back in the fifties in one of the more pristine areas of the Green Mountains, and has been tinkering with it ever since.

The focal point of all Smith's plans was Mount Killington itself. At more than 4,000 feet on National Forest land, it is one of the highest peaks in Vermont.

Within a few years, Killington had added lifts to two smaller peaks next to Mount Killington - Snowdon and Rams Head – which empty skiers into the same meadow. These lift systems, along with lifts on the shoulder of Mount Killington, provided all the terrain necessary to keep skiers of all abilities happy.

There is an entire mountain, Snowshed, devoted to beginners, and a number of peaks – Bear Mountain (3,296 feet), Killington (4,241 feet) and Skye Peak (3,800 feet) – serving the more expert skier. Snowshed and Skye Peak have both benefited from the introduction recently of new high-speed 'quad' chairs.

But what really set Killington apart from the rest of the world of east-coast skiing was the construction of the four-mile gondola along a flank of Mount Killington which extended down much lower than the resort base and its other lifts. This meant that Killington could now boast the longest gondola in the country, a 3,000-foot vertical drop, a new four-mile run as well as its supreme snow-making facilities.

A decade later, Smith was still intent on expanding. The next addition, for expert skiers, was a rich new golden vein to plunder or an awe-inspiring and fearsome challenge, depending on your point of view. Bear Mountain – with the steepest gradient in the east (sixty-two degrees) was opened up. Then came the next phase, Sunrise Mountain and the Northeast Passage Base. Experts will thrive on the steep terrain of Outer Limits (the steepest mogul slope in New England) and the Devil's Fiddle.

Beginners and novice intermediates will adore the Juggernaut – a blissful ten-mile cruise from top to bottom. Imagine the excitement of a rawish beginner being able to tell the 'folks back home' that he or she has conquered what is claimed to be America's longest run. Almost half (forty-five per cent) of the skiing is suitable for beginners, twenty per cent for intermediates and the rest (thirty-five per cent) is considered good for experts. The skiing is from 1,060 feet up to 4,241 feet.

On one memorable day in 1987, more than eighteen thousand people turned up to ski Killington – more than at any other ski area in the whole of the USA, including Vail and Mammoth. During the following winter, (1988–89) two new high-speed detachable 'quad' chairs were installed – the Superstar to Skye Peak and the Snowshed III. The resort also added five new trails and bought five new snow-grooming machines giving it a total of eighteen. The area is vast and fortunately very well sign-posted, often with visual *aides-mémoires* that match the name of the trails, such as Ram's Head, or Bear.

Killington is already the biggest and best of the East Coast resorts. I suspect it is going to get bigger. And hopefully – even better.

MAMMOTH/June

The urban sprawl of the Los Angeles basin may be a seven-hour drive away, but during weekends at Mammoth – if it were not for the snow – you could easily be under the impression that you were backed up at a red light on a Hollywood boulevard.

There are far worse places to be stuck in a traffic jam. The scenery is so stunning that it is in some ways a relief to have time to gaze at it. The

The hurly-burly of Los Angeles seems a million miles away.

backdrop of the craggy Minaret peaks in the Sierra Nevada range or the desolate Mono Lake accompanied by glimpses of Death Valley should keep boredom at a fairly high threshold. This – as its name suggests – huge ski area claims to sell more lift passes than any other resort in the USA. Something like fourteen thousand skiers are in the resort at weekends. And yet very few skiers venture there from Europe. Rather than serving an overseas market, Mammoth is predominantly a short-haul destination resort principally serving Californians. It is the closest major resort to Los Angeles, which unfortunately encourages the irritating traffic jams on the approach roads and serious lift-line queues.

Mammoth is based around what the Americans claim, rather alarmingly, is a 'barely dormant volcano.' The lift map area is so big that it is more like an atlas. There are three thousand acres of skiable terrain, one hundred and fifty trails, thirty-two lifts, two gondolas, and four tows. The resort, with a summit of more than 11,000 feet and a vertical drop of more than 3,000 vertical feet, catches enough snow to stay open later than any other Californian ski resort. The skiing can, in theory, last until 4th July, or even later.

There is some excellent bowl and chute skiing from the top of Gondola Two. And, like so many American resorts soon to face the challenge of the nineties, Mammoth is 'into' quad chairs. They have finally replaced Chair One – Mammoth's first lift, built in 1955 – with their first quad.

Mammoth is undoubtedly a 'world-class' mountain with a good snow record, and is certainly an attractive prospect for the indigenous Californian population. Although the snow can be bountiful (a storm wafting in from the Pacific can dump five feet of snow in the Sierras in one night) it does not come from the same high-class stable as the kind that falls in Utah and Colorado. Because it has no desert to 'blow dry' it, Californian snow is wetter and there is some substance to rival states' claims that at its worst it can be likened to 'Sierra Cement.'

As my American skiing adviser and collaborator Joe Kirwin says, 'The Pacific Ocean is one hell of a mortar mixer but the water-laden fall-out is not exactly a skier's delight.' Fortunately Californian snow is by no means always in this category.

Mammoth Mountain – the big one . . . California's most popular ski resort.

Some Mammoth veterans maintain that it would not matter if it were Sierra 'cement' or 'crazy glue' on the higher slopes because there is sufficient vertical drop on trails that lead off the celebrated Mammoth Cornice between Gondola Two and Chair Twenty-three for you to be able to turn the longest and most obstinate of skis.

This ridge – with trails such as Climax, Drop Out and Wipe Out – is one of the principal reasons why experts keep renewing their season passes. About thirty per cent of Mammoth's skiing is considered to be expert terrain and another forty per cent is deemed suitable for intermediates. On the lower part of the mountain, Broadway and Stump Alley are probably the most popular, and best avoided during the 'rush hour' period before and after lunch. Beginners will enjoy trails such as Jill's Run or Sesame Street.

Despite the size of Mammoth, it is still something of a family resort. Indeed it is one of the last major resorts still actually *run* by a family. Dave McCoy started Mammoth back in the late forties with one lift and has supervized its growth ever since. To this day you can still find him riding the lifts and talking to skiers who give him ideas for the continuing development of the resort.

Mammoth has a 'second season' – from 1st May to 4th July – when skiers can enjoy excellent 'corn' (spring) snow, often described as similar to skiing on fine ball-bearings. During this period most things, including lift passes, are cheaper. Some skiers find that corn snow produces the most enjoyable conditions of the year.

Mammoth is linked with June Mountain, just twenty-five minutes away via Highway 395 and Route 158. A new high-speed aerial tram (cable car) has just been built there, which takes just four minutes to reach The June Meadows Chalet. From here you have a choice of going to the summit of June (10,135 feet) or Ranbow (10,050 feet.)

June Mountain also has a detachable quad as well as five double chairs and more than thirty runs of its own. The vertical drop is around 2,590 feet, and the average snowfall is 250 inches.

Mammoth/June may not be a resort on the itineraries of many European skiers, but without it a lot of businessmen and their families in California and neighbouring states would be rather unhappy people.

SKI FACTS

	MAMMOTH
TRAILS	150+
EASIEST	30%
MORE DIFFICULT	40%
MOST DIFFICULT	30%
PEAK ELEVATION	11,000 ft
VERTICAL DROP	3,100 ft
GONDOLAS	2
CHAIR LIFTS	25 (3 quads, 7 triples and 15 doubles)
TOWS	5
AVERAGE SNOWFALL	335 in
	JUNE
TRAILS	30+
EASIEST	35%
MORE DIFFICULT	45%
MOST DIFFICULT	20%
PEAK ELEVATION	10,135 ft
VERTICAL DROP	2,590 ft
TRAMS	1
CHAIR LIFTS	6 (1 quad and 5 doubles)
AVERAGE SNOWFALL	250 in

PARK CITY

Many people rave about Park City, and I wish I were one of them. But unfortunately I don't really enjoy the look of the place, and it's not its fault. The skiing is good – indeed since 1973 it has been the home of the American ski team.

You cannot improve on the famous 'freeze-dried' Utah powder. As for the people, they could not have been more friendly. Twenty-five years ago, the place was virtually unknown. Now it is the largest skiing area in Utah: 2,200 acres of skiing, more than eighty-two trails, fourteen lifts (includ-

ing the longest four-passenger gondola in the American West) a vertical drop of over three-thousand feet, and one of the longest floodlit night-skiing runs in the Rockies. It is even 'twinned' with the choicest of French resorts, Courchevel.

But scenically, it has certain disadvantages. The

resort is built on hundreds of miles of old silver-mine workings, and the hills and mountains in this part of Utah's Wasatch Forest have a rounded, grey, almost industrial feeling about them. Many of the trees are Aspens, which unlike fir trees lose their foliage in winter which gives them a rather lack-lustre, bleak, unfriendly appearance. The overall effect is a little drab, grey and rather ugly – in total contrast with Park City's near neighbour Snowbird which, with its alpine peaks and fresh green spruces and firs, positively sparkles by comparison. Unfortunately this led to my being much happier skiing in Snowbird than Park City.

However, there is nothing wrong with Park City's skiing, and it would be churlish, not to mention inaccurate to omit it from this book just because it does not appeal to me aesthetically.

Off the slopes, Park City has one major attraction that almost makes up for its drabness elsewhere: Main Street. It's a gem. Some sixty-four of the original old mining buildings have been listed in America's National Register of Historic Places. These are delightfully interspersed with carefully reproduced replicas. In all, there are fifty shops and galleries, eighteen bars and private clubs and forty-five restaurants in the space of a little over two miles.

Although technically it is difficult to get a drink in Utah, they seem to bend the rules. Indeed it is often recalled that back in the mining days, not a single man had been known to start at the top of the town, take a drink in every bar, and make it to the bottom still standing.

To wander along this street today is to be transported back a century to the days when the mining community was still thriving. It still feels uncannily like the real thing.

At its peak, Park City was the site of the largest silver-mining camp in the entire country, with a population of ten thousand. More than four

Leafless aspens and abandoned mining relics – all part of Park City's atmospheric skiing.

aires, including George Hearst, founder of the Hearst mining and newspaper dynasty, and father of William Randolph Hearst whose niece Patricia caused the family such embarrassment by becoming an urban guerrilla for a while.

One of the main problems in mining the silver was that the workings were very wet. Huge pumps had to be installed, based on those built in Cornwall, to be used in the deep, wet diamond mines of South Africa. When the biggest of these froze one year, the desperate workers called in a Cornish mechanic. What happened next is documented in Park City's tourist magazine, *Lodestar*:

> The Cornishman eyed the stubborn engine, climbed its towering flywheel and struck it a single , ringing blow with a sledge-hammer. The huge machine shuddered into action. To the chagrin of his superiors, he billed them $100 for this simple act. When an itemized bill was demanded, the mechanic wrote:
> For hitting the flywheel with the hammer, 50 cents.
> For knowing where to hit it, $99:50.
> He was paid his fee.

hundred million dollars of silver ore was eventually taken out of mines on Jupiter Peak. The first silver strike came in 1868, when two soldiers found silver-bearing ore in a canyon on the eastern slope of the Wasatch range. A handful of prospectors' tents sprang up, but it was not until four years later, when a Rector Steen came upon an outcropping of almost pure silver in Ontario Canyon that the silver rush began in earnest. Less than a decade later, more than five thousand people had moved there. To quote the local tourist office, they created 'a wonderful mixture of precariously perched homes, false-fronted shops, smokey saloons, theatres, churches, a red-light district and a Chinatown.' Park City became the site of the largest silver-mining camp in the entire country.

Over the next fifty years or so, hundreds of mines were started, thousands of miles of tunnels were bored and twenty-three men became million-

At about this time, Norwegian immigrants searching for silver introduced the locals to the pleasures of gliding through the snow on boards cut from hickory which were strapped to their shoes with leather thongs. It was a distant precursor of a new boom.

Today, with Salt Lake City and its airport (served by forty-seven North American cities) a mere twenty-seven miles away, people are flocking to stake their claim to some good skiing. Even the road which takes you there – the Interstate 1–80 – has been 're-christened' Winterstate-80.

Salt Lake City itself – the headquarters of the Church of Jesus Christ of the Latter Day Saints (Mormons) – is fascinating to visit, with its many-spired Mormon temple and 'turtle-back' Tabernacle, which was built in the 1860s without a single nail. It contains the world-famous organ with 10,700 pipes.

Salt Lake's streets were made specially wide to enable the Mormons' leader, Brigham Young, to turn his covered wagons round easily. To this day the majority of the population remains Mormon.

Main Street – memories of the silver-mining community.

No doubt, there are many in the ski resort of Park City. Young could hardly have guessed that many of his latter-day followers would end up running a ski resort.

Almost half of Park City's eighty-two runs are for intermediates. But like its neighbour, Snowbird, Park City has some fabulous bowl skiing – 650 acres in Jupiter, Scott, McConkey, Blue Slip and Puma Bowls.

There is floodlit skiing every night on the one-and-a-quarter-mile intermediate run, Payday (claimed to be the longest floodlit run in the Rockies) and First Time, a novice trail. You can also go helicopter skiing, and experience the hugely enjoyable Interconnect off-piste ski tour linking up with Brighton, Solitude, Alta and Snowbird (see under Snowbird.)

Park City's skiing ranges from 6,900 feet to 10,007 feet – about a thousand feet lower than Snowbird. Many of the eighty-two or more runs inevitably reflect the town's strong mining origins: Pick 'n Shovel, Bonanza, Motherlode, Prospector and Claimjumper. The best runs for more advanced skiers include Silver Skis, The Hoist, The Shaft and Glory Hole.

The first site for a ski resort was called Snow Park, today the site of the neighbouring resort of Deer Valley. Park West opened in 1968 and Deer Valley as recently as 1981.

Salt Lake is ringed with seven good skiing areas in three canyons: Park City, Deer Valley, and Park West in Parley's Canyon; Brighton and Solitude in Big Cottonwood Canyon; and Alta and Snowbird in Little Cottonwood Canyon.

Although the snow in Utah is rated as the finest in the world, it does not always distribute its bounty in fair portions. One canyon might get a foot – the next almost nothing.

Many skiers, agree with Peter Oliver, of the *American Skiing Magazine*, who advocates staying in Salt Lake City itself rather than committing himself to any specific resort. That way, he can follow the best snow on a day-to-day basis. This is how he suggests getting the best out of the cavalierish Utah snow-falls: 'The sun is up, spilling its light over Millcreek Canyon, the narrow slip between Parley's and Big Cottonwood. The man on the radio says its nearly fifty degrees already, and half the city is still in bed.

'The man also gives me a canyon report. A snow hiccup has left six fresh inches in Big Cottonwood, so I toss my skiing tackle into the back of the jeep and head for Solitude.

'The first axiom of the urban ski bum's life: go with the snow!'

SKI FACTS

TRAILS	82 (2,200 acres)
EASIEST	17%
MORE DIFFICULT	49%
MOST DIFFICULT	34%
PEAK ELEVATION	10,000 ft
VERTICAL DROP	3,100 ft
GONDOLAS	1 4-passenger
CHAIR LIFTS	13 (8 doubles and 5 triples)
TOWS	1
AVERAGE SNOWFALL	350 in

Park City Ski Area

SNOWBIRD

U tah! One of those words like Aspen, that gets skiers and wild-west enthusiasts instantly excited. If Aspen is the buzz word for skiing atmosphere, Utah is the trigger word for every serious skier's dream: Powder.

Utah powder is the best you can get. They call it the Greatest Snow on Earth. The Pacific clouds are dried out as they cross the west coast deserts and then they come hurtling in over the Wasatch Mountains in great storms and dump it by the fluffiest of mega-tons. The target these powder storms seem to favour most is that most thorough-bred of resorts, Snowbird.

With its 1,900 acres of skiing, Snowbird had the benefit of careful planning when it was built in the late sixties. Unlike most resorts which evolved from existing villages not necessarily situated in the best snow areas, and certainly unlike most other American resorts, Snowbird was built in the tradition of the French purpose-built resorts and has even been loosely compared with Flaine.

Dick Bass, the Texan oilman who built it, selected a site in Little Cottonwood Canyon (7,900 feet) from which Mormon pioneers once quarried granite for the construction of their temple in Salt Lake City. The canyon is not only very beautiful but also attracts huge snowfalls. Thus the resort has no delusions of modesty when assessing itself against the attractions of its rival ski resorts. It sees itself as a skiing version of Liverpool Football Club, generally topping the league in most seasons.

The Snowbird marketing department believes the resort's snow record is so spectacular that there is no contest. They claim 550 inches a year, more

Snowbird shares the deepest and lightest snow in America with its neighbour Alta.

than twice as much as Aspen and Sun Valley, and a third more than Jackson Hole, Squaw Valley, Park City and Steamboat Springs. (Their rivals dispute these figures.) However, there seems little doubt that Snowbird does usually receive the heaviest snowfalls of any American ski resort.

Snowbird also claims a season lasting 212 days: the 'rest', they say, can only manage between 120 to 156. And the resort is also most keen to point out its proximity to a major international airport. It is only thirty-one miles from Salt Lake City. This compares with Jackson Hole, which is 275 miles. Note the following distances from Denver to the main Colorado ski resorts: Aspen 208 miles; Vail 107; Steamboat Springs 172. Sun Valley is 150 miles from Boise. Some of these figures are misleading, however, because there are perfectly good local (if not 'international') airports serving Jackson Hole, Aspen and Steamboat Springs.

However, it is true to claim that depending where 'home' is you can in theory leave it in the morning and be skiing Snowbird the same afternoon. With undisguised arrogance, Snowbird's image-makers say: 'knowledgeable skiers don't settle for five-to-six-hour car rides' to experience Eastern boilerplate or Sierra cement!'

They are a little smug about their resort, but they do have a lot to be proud of. It is certainly a beautiful place, with superb forests of Engelmann spruce, ponderosa and lodgepole pine, Douglas fir and some fabulous skiing.

Compared with Vail and Jackson Hole its only shortcoming perhaps is that there is not quite enough of it. However, extending the resort into White Pine Valley will add a large and welcome new area. Dick Bass – a former oil executive famous for climbing the 'seven continents' highest peaks in his fifties – wants to expand over towards Twin Peaks in the direction of Robert Redford's Sundance resort. 'It is my greatest dream to expand Snowbird to twenty-four square miles', he told me as we got off the tram in a blizzard of almost perfect Utah powder during my last visit in February 1989.

Although the 'village' itself unfortunately tends towards the modern, clinical, concrete concept of many purpose-built resorts, Snowbird is what so many ski resorts claim to be but usually do not quite live up to – a genuine ski paradise.

It is very proud of its tram, said to be the fastest in America, which takes 125 people at a time speeding up to the summit of Hidden Peak (11,000 feet) in eight minutes (seven if you read different literature). From there you ski an exhilarating three-thousand-foot vertical drop or traverse to some excellent bowl and chute skiing in Peruvian Gulch or Gad Valley. As an alternative to the tram, you can take the Little Cloud lift which offers you much the same terrain except that it does not quite reach the same height as the tram.

When they are open, Great Scott, Upper Cirque and Gad Chutes are among the finest out-of-bounds runs you could find, expecially in powder. But even in 'crud' – which in America merely means ungroomed rather than 'gorilla snow,' the ankle-wrenching European version – they are so exhila-

The Snowbird marketing department likes to see the name in high places.

rating that your ski host cannot restrain a whoop of joy. One of my favourite runs – quirky and steep – is called Mark Malu Fork. Gadzooks, Tiger Tail and Carbonate are other good black runs.

For intermediates and advancing beginners, Big Emma is one of the finest and widest trails in America.

Snowbird is one of the starting points for a memorable out-of-bounds tour in 'the boonies' called the Interconnect. This takes in the neighbouring resorts of Alta (one of America's original ski areas), Solitude and Brighton, or a longer version which starts from Park City.

Wearing avalanche bleepers and profoundly anxious after a pre-tour lecture about avalanches, your small party of a dozen or less, plus two guides equipped with walkie-talkie radios, sets out early. Off the pisted track, you can all enjoy the peace and solitude of cruising through woods and snow-covered pastures with the special cameraderie that seems to envelop small groups of skiers exploring the snowy wilds and backwoods together.

(To be brutally honest, there was not too much peace for one slightly breathless, chubby, moustachioed young member of the group who made the mistake of wearing a label on his ski-suit which proclaimed: 'NO GUTS, NO GLORY.' This was too much for our chief guide Ray Santa Maria to resist and the unfortunate chap was thereafter referred to as 'No Guts.' He took it in good spirits.)

After reaching the beautiful ridge overlooking the Heber Valley and the distant Uinta Mountains, you traverse Point Supreme over to Catherine's Pass overlooking the resort of Brighton.

After skiing down via Catherine's Bowl to Brighton, it is over to Solitude via the Solbright trail. After lunch, Sunrise and Summit lifts take you to the highlight of the tour – scenically if not in terms of the actual skiing. A seemingly endless traverse called Highway to Heaven, takes you to Twin Lakes Pass and on through the trees in Grizzly Gulch down to Alta.

Because of the danger of avalanches on Highway to Heaven, each skier must wait for the one in front to ski the critical section alone before following. This minimizes the chances of an avalanche sweeping the entire party away. In spite of the danger, the organizers have not lost a single skier since they started these tours in the seventies.

'Anyone seen No Guts?' squawked Santa Maria affectionately into his radio. The guide, taking up the rear, was asking his colleague who had skied the traverse first to check the conditions. No Guts had temporarily and nervously disappeared from view round a rock a quarter of a mile away. After a few moments' uneasy pause, the reply crackled back: 'Yeh – here he is now. Hi, No Guts! How ya doin'?'

No Guts, it seems, had found some guts after all. But he was rather relieved, at the end of the day, to put the backwoods behind him, and ski back once more on the glorious and rather less unsettling slopes of sunny Snowbird.

Of Snowbird's magnificent 1,900 acres of skiing, twenty per cent is said to be suitable for beginners, thirty per cent for intermediates and the rest is there to be plundered by experts.

It is pure joy to ski there – whatever your ability.

SKI FACTS

TRAILS	32 (1,900 acres)
EASIEST	20%
MORE DIFFICULT	30%
MOST DIFFICULT	50%
PEAK ELEVATION	11,000 ft
VERTICAL DROP	3,100 ft
TRAMS	1 125-passenger
CHAIR LIFTS	7 doubles
ANNUAL SNOWFALL	550 in

snowbird
ski and summer resort

SNOWMASS

S nowmass has been described as 'a breathtaking blend of Southern Californian convenience and Rocky Mountain ruggedness.' It is not a bad description.

Everyone has heard of Aspen, its next-door neighbour. But Snowmass, although bigger, still lives slightly in its shadow. Located in the White River National Forest, it is two hundred miles south-west of Denver.

When I first visited Snowmass in 1978 it was the first time I had skied in America. While the concept was most exciting, subsequent visits to Aspen, Vail and the Lake Tahoe resorts in California/Nevada persuaded me that there was not an awful lot to write home about concerning the skiing at Snowmass. Having just returned, however, I find that now there is.

Alone in the trees – they thrive as high as 10,000 feet in America.

Opposite
A giant leap for mankind – we'll never know whether he made it!

SKI FACTS

TRAILS	84
	55 miles (1,580 acres)
EASIEST	9%
MORE DIFFICULT	51%
MOST DIFFICULT	18%
EXPERT	22%
PEAK ELEVATION	11,835 ft
VERTICAL DROP	3,615 ft
LONGEST RUN	$4\frac{1}{4}$ miles
CHAIR LIFTS	14 (3 quads, 2 triples and 9 doubles)
TOWS	2
ANNUAL SNOWFALL	300 in

Just twelve miles down the road from its famous neighbour Aspen – and linked by a free bus shuttle – Snowmass has, until recently, had a reputation for being a fairly bland, family-orientated ski resort.

Things have changed.

Every year they are adding on whole new areas of excitement to what is already one of the largest ski areas in America: they are carving some really challenging runs out of the surrounding terrain. The expansion of Burnt Mountain, for example, between Snowmass and Buttermilk, will open up nine hundred acres of excellent intermediate and advanced skiing. Little by little – and sometimes by quite substantial amounts – Snowmass is being transformed from a bland resort to a breathtaking one. It is already rivalling Aspen in its quest to be crowned as the most important ski resort in the valley. The old master is under attack from the parvenu.

The Aspen Skiing Company has even moved its headquarters to Snowmass, which now has almost as many skiers as the other three resorts put together.

In the old days, when Snowmass was merely a satellite of Aspen, it used to be called Snowmass-at-Aspen. Nowadays it sits proudly on its own as just Snowmass, and is in danger of dwarfing its celebrated neighbour ... although I doubt whether Aspen's pride will ever allow it to be called Aspen-at-Snowmass!

The skiing area at Snowmass is vast – so vast that as in resorts such as Val d'Isère, or, closer to home, Jackson Hole, you could ski here for a week without ever skiing the same run twice. They even open the lifts half an hour earlier here – at 8.30 am – to give you a fighting chance of getting round to as much of the skiing as possible.

In spite of all the changes, its most famous run remains Big Burn, a wide ridge often packed with powder, which extends for 4.16 miles all the way down to Fanny Hill. In places it is almost a mile across. It was called Big Burn partly because it was originally created by a forest fire – and partly because skiers come scorching down it at great speed.

Like so many Colorado resorts, the skiing here is high, ranging from 8,220 feet up to 11,775 feet (vertical drop 3,615 feet). There are sixteen lifts, including three 'quad' Super Chairs (American for fast) two triples and nine doubles. The uphill capacity is 20,535 skiers an hour. And there are eighty-four trails spread over 1,582 acres for them to enjoy. There is even a reduced rate for lift passes if you are over sixty-five. Aspen offers the same facility and people aged seventy or more can actually ski for nothing at the neighbouring resort of Buttermilk!

Snowmass was built during nine months in 1967 with the aid of a computer which 'measured' the mountain on a projected skiers-per-acre basis. It was a clever idea: they decided that one acre would accommodate, or 'absorb' five experts, ten intermediates or fifteen beginners! The resort claims as much as fifty-one per cent of its terrain is in the 'more difficult' category, with only nine per cent alloted for the 'easiest' standard. This should not deter beginners because in my view their definition of 'more difficult' is a trifle over stated. It really is an excellent resort for improving beginners and intermediates. The 'most difficult' category is said to be eighteen per cent with twenty-two per cent classified as 'expert.' Snow-making equipment covers fifty-five acres.

One of the main themes of Snowmass is that you can ski in and ski out of just about everywhere. There is even ski-in and ski-out shopping and ski-in and ski-out apres ski!

Not just Big Burn, but the rolling slopes of Elk Camp, the bumps at Campground and the challenging faces of Hanging Valley are on your doorstep. Although Snowmass is a paradise for intermediates, new areas are being opened up to attract the experts too. Hanging Valley is one of its toughest new areas at the moment, but each winter new areas are promised, so it looks as though I shall have to keep skiing Snowmass every year to keep up with the changes!

Like all the other ski resorts in America, Snowmass has some wonderfully evocatively named runs, such as: Sam's Knob, Whispering Jess, Powderhorn, Sheer Bliss, Garret Gulch, Glissade, Naked Lady, Turkey Trot and Bear Bottom. And, of course, the superlatives at Snowmass are – to use one – endless: highest ... biggest ... widest.

Anyone who has not yet skied in America could do a lot worse than make a start at Snowmass, Colorado. It is rather good.

SQUAW VALLEY

holiday-makers take advantage of this to see a 'big-name' show or indulge in a little gambling.

The valley was discovered as long ago as AD 500 by the Washoe Indians who gave it its name. But it was not until 1863 that rumours of vast silver deposits brought people flocking to the scene. But by 1865, that particular dream was already over. Although many of America's ski resorts started out as mining towns, that was not to be Squaw Valley's experience. 'No Silver Found . . .' reads the terse information sheet in front of me.

Instead, Squaw became a farming and lumbering community. It was only after the Second World War that skiing started to take over.

By 1949 Squaw Valley ski resort had opened with Squaw Valley Lodge, plus what is claimed to have been the world's first double chair lift, and two pony tows. By 1955 Squaw's future was assured. It had been chosen as the site for the eighth Winter Olympics in 1960. At the opening ceremony – orchestrated by Walt Disney – the sun burst through stormy skies as two thousand pigeons soared above the mountain peaks, followed by a kaleidoscope of fireworks and balloons. The music was provided by fifty-two school bands, 2,645 voices and 1,285 instruments. These were the first Winter Olympics to use computerized results and artificial refrigeration for the skating events.

Squaw had twenty feet of snow before the games, but most of it was washed away by rain. Another twelve feet fell just before the games started. By the time it was all over, the thousand Olympians had set an official new record of their own: they had consumed ten tons of meat between them.

Today the old Olympic Village has now been replaced by luxurious condominiums. But the mountains are still there. And what mountains!

There is skiing on the broad flanks of six peaks in the High Sierras – Red Dog, Emigrant, Squaw Peak, Granite Chief, Broken Arrow and perhaps the toughest of all, the legendary, somewhat fearsome KT-22. These are served by almost thirty lifts, including a 150-passenger aerial tram – one of the biggest in the world.

The resort claims that there is little queuing – and even offers free skiing for the rest of the day should lift lines cause an average of more than ten minutes' delay. Squaw claims over 450 inches of snow a season. (Snowbird claims this should

Much more of a Brave than a Squaw, Squaw Valley is the biggest, toughest and arguably the best of nineteen resorts built around the beautiful Lake Tahoe, a breathtaking stretch of cobalt-blue water twenty-four miles long between California and Nevada.

Squaw is vast (8,300 acres) and a little frightening in outlook. It has an atmosphere of slight foreboding, and sometimes reminds me of Chamonix, where I feel a similar tingle in my spine – partly of pleasant anticipation, partly of anxiety.

Squaw, 'twinned' with Val d'Isere and Joetsu Kokusai (Japan) is marketed as 'the ski resort of the 21st century.' Quite why is unclear. Perhaps we shall discover the answer in January 2000. Squaw is not far from the Nevada border, and some

Condominiums have taken the place of the old Olympic Village.

Previous page
Squaw Valley is Lake Tahoe's toughest ski area.

read 300 ... but then they would, wouldn't they?)

Although Squaw has the toughest skiing in the Sierras – big cliffs, big 'steeps' and big bumps – it has a surprising number of runs suitable for beginners – something like twenty-five per cent. But its reputation world-wide is as a big tough, challenging ski resort. Like Jackson Hole, it has perhaps been oversold on its difficult slopes rather than its easy ones. Forty-five per cent is rated as suitable for intermediates, leaving thirty per cent for expert skiers.

According to the *American Skiing Magazine*, the 'manicured low-angle pastures of the Gold Coast and the Mainline draw ten times more skiers than KT-22's advanced and expert West Faces, and a thousand times more skiers than the dreaded cliffs above Siberia Bowl.'

If you are keen enough to ski down the back of KT-22 to the neighbouring resort of Alpine Meadows, you have to 'sign out' before you leave, and what is more, telephone to say you have arrived safely.

Squaw's skiing is divided into two main areas – one starts at 6,200 feet, the other at 8,200. The vertical drop is 2,700 feet and the skiing can be as high as 9,000 feet. Unlike most other ski resorts (except Heavenly Valley and one or two others) Squaw's main beginners' slopes are on *top* of the mountain rather than at the bottom. This means a rare treat for novices – being able to get up there among the peaks and enjoy the stunning scenery like 'real' skiers. This makes a pleasant change from having to labour on beginners' slopes round the corner from their hotel in town, possibly without the faintest idea from Day One until they return home what skiing is really all about.

Some of Squaw's easiest lifts (Bailey's Beach, Links and Belmont) are on gentle, meadow-like slopes at the top of the cable car. The view – which includes Lake Tahoe in the distance – is superb.

Like many American resorts, Squaw encourages night-time skiing. Both the Searchlight and Exhibition trails are illuminated for three nights a week.

Because the skiing area is so huge, the largest collection of snow-cats in the Tahoe region – almost thirty of them – is required to flatten trails throughout the night, seven days a week during the season. When rocks begin to peep through the surface of the melting snow late in the spring, they are painted red. Then when the snow has finally disappeared beneath the Californian sun, the rocks are flattened and removed.

Squaw Valley, like its reputation, is big. The skiing is exciting and sometimes almost over-powering. In spite of its good beginners' slopes, the resort as a whole does not suffer fools gladly. Like Chamonix, it is considerably larger than life and it is eminently sensible to treat it with the greatest of respect.

SKI FACTS

TRAILS	Open-bowl skiing (8,300 acres)
EASIEST	25%
MORE DIFFICULT	45%
MOST DIFFICULT	30%
PEAK ELEVATION	9,050 ft
VERTICAL DROP	2,850 ft
TRAMS	1 150-passenger
GONDOLAS	1 6-passenger
CHAIR LIFTS	23 (2 quads, 5 triples and 16 doubles)
TOWS	2
AVERAGE SNOWFALL	450 in

SQUAW VALLEY USA

STOWE

They say it is cold on the East Coast. Very cold. It is. Long Johns are not a suggestion: they are an order. And face masks and boot muffs are not a bad idea either. But this is no reason not to enjoy the skiing at one of America's pioneer ski resorts.

Indeed, Stowe folk will swear till they are blue in the face – if they are not already – that with the advent of the high-speed quadruple chair, which is the buzz-word for uphill transportation in America, plus artificial snow cannons and better trail-grooming techniques, the 'icy and nightmarish' skiing that once typified Stowe in March is a thing of the past.

If you are from New York, Boston, Washington DC or from anywhere in New England, you have to be fairly dedicated or rich to jet across to the other side of America just to get warmer – and admittedly, usually longer – skiing.

Of course you do not get the powder here that you can in Utah, Wyoming or Colorado, where the snow is 'freeze-dried' as it flurries across the Nevada desert. And of course skiers from the East Coast *do* sometimes think it worth travelling all that way even if they have got snow – or Stowe – on their doorstep. But it can also happen in reverse. I remember in the winter of 1986/87 people were scrambling from the West Coast to the East because for once the snow was better over there. In either case, it is certainly a myth that the skiing on America's East Coast is just something to play at in between *real* skiing in the West or in the Alps. You only have to stand at the base at Stowe and look up at the famous 'double-black diamond' (blacker-than-black) Front Four descents – or, even more intimidatingly, look *down* them.

Dropping straight down at a thirty-six-degree gradient off the face of Mount Mansfield, Vermont's highest peak, with a 2,350-foot vertical drop, these runs are four good reasons why the natives of Stowe do not have even a hint of a skiing inferiority

Mount Mansfield: 'soothes the beginner, challenges the intermediate and knocks the wind from the lungs of experts'.

complex. If you can manage runs like National, Starr or Goat, you can 'point' em' (your skis) down the mountain virtually anywhere in the world. And that applies too to Liftline, where you are guaranteed an audience as you swing or subside in the moguls. As its name suggests, it is right beneath the gaze of uphill travellers seeking to amuse themselves at your expense. The moguls – especially at the top where they are steepest – do not really help to boost one's confidence. Goat is probably the toughest of the four, but at least here you can make a fool of yourself in relative privacy.

These runs are all about a mile long, so there is no easy or quick way of avoiding the difficulties. And lift-ride for lift-ride, you can enjoy as much skiing at Stowe as you will in most European or Rocky Mountain resorts.

People have been skiing Stowe for longer than they have skied Sun Valley – even before the First World War. Today it has almost fifty trails served by five lifts. The skiing reaches 4,393 feet with a vertical drop of 2,350 feet.

Skiers wanting something a little less testing could try the fierce-sounding but now tamed Nosedive – once a terror to ski, but after a cosmetic reconstruction, now more of a cruise. The management was hoping that this might attract more intermediate skiers. Perhaps the name could be changed now too. It would certainly help psychologically!

From Nosedive, you can ski off to the right where the locals used to covet some excellent tree-skiing. Snow would often blow into this area and remain for days. Recently some of the trees have been removed to make way for some new trails which have been cut, but it remains a good area for powder.

It looks cosy and snug and it needs to be. Stowe is not the warmest place on earth.

Nosedive also provides access to the Gondola area, the gentler side of Mount Mansfield, now that many of the slopes have been made less fierce in recent seasons. What used to be steep, narrow, zig-zagging chutes (couloirs) have been transformed into open, cruising slopes with snow-making equipment close at hand to keep the ice at bay. But others, such as Chin Clip, still rated as a slope for experts, are reminders of what some of these trails used to be like before their fangs were removed.

Centreline and Hayride, though officially listed as double-black diamonds, are not as severe as that category suggests. And for even blander but still exciting skiing, Skimeister and Sunride provide excellent cruising trails.

Spruce Peak (1,550-foot vertical drop) – across the street from the Quad and Gondola slopes - has twelve trails and four double-chairs, and can provide artificial snow on sixty-five of its runs (it will eventually be one hundred per cent). This is the mountain most suitable for beginners and intermediates, but there is also some excellent tree-skiing for the more skilful skier.

There is even a double-chair – Easy Street – which operates especially slowly for beginners just learning how to ride a chair.

At the other extreme, a strong novice would enjoy runs like the Sterling Trail – beginners need challenging runs too! From Spruce Peak it is also possible to ski over to Smuggler's Notch, another ski resort.

Snow-making equipment has reduced some of the premier 'boiler-plate' or ocean-blue ice that used to exist in Stowe, but there are still days when it pays to have your edges razor sharp.

It was a few immigrant Swedes who really started spreading the skiing bug here when they began walking around on skis back in 1913. Local enthusiasts enjoying the 'great outdoors' followed suit and began skiing on Mount Mansfield back in the twenties. They had to hike four and a half miles up the mountain Toll Road.

The real development at Stowe started in the early thirties, when a financier, Roland Palmedo, persuaded New York's Amateur Ski Club that it could be as good a ski mountain as anything the Europeans had to offer. So the Civilian Conservation Corps got down to work and began to cut the trails. Many of them are still in use today.

Mansfield was the location for the first chair lift to be installed in the east. (It was only replaced in 1986.) When it opened in 1940, it was also America's biggest vertical drop. According to the tourist office, Mansfield 'soothes the beginner, challenges the intermediate, and knocks the wind from the lungs of confident experts.'

Despite all the development over the last decade or so in Stowe, there is often an old world charm and New England flavour that symbolizes small-town Yankee hospitality.

Even the Trapp Family Lodge – depicted in the film *The Sound of Music* – has been 'resurrected' in spirit after being burnt down in 1980. The new and luxurious building erected there is hardly the same as the original but somehow seems to symbolize, in a very cosy way, the successful meld of new and old world that thrives at Stowe.

SKI FACTS

TRAILS	44 (578 acres)
EASIEST	19%
MORE DIFFICULT	48%
MOST DIFFICULT	33%
PEAK ELEVATION	4,393 ft
VERTICAL DROP	2,350 ft
GONDOLAS	1
CHAIR LIFTS	8 (1 quad, 1 triple and 6 doubles)
AVERAGE SNOWFALL	250 in

MOUNT
MANSFIELD

SUN VALLEY

Sun Valley, another Grande Dame of American ski resorts is, they say, like Paris – sooner or later, you just have to go there. It claims to be the oldest ski resort in America (it all depends on whether you consider a ski resort to have 'started' with its first ski-lift or before) and some aficionados say it is still the best. It is steep by nature and as steeped in history as any American winter sports area can be – a ski area before most people in the States had even heard of skiing.

The man behind it was the celebrated Averell Harriman, chairman of the Union Pacific Railroad. He spent a million pounds to build the resort for one quite basic reason – to promote more winter business for his railroad company. 'Only an American millionaire could have done this!' chanted the British *Sunday Dispatch* on 21st August 1938. To build his 'new Tyrol' Harriman had the vital assistance of Count Felix Schaffgotsch when he looked for a suitable site for both skiing and easy access to a railhead.

But the Tyrol they created in Idaho bore more resemblance to Hollywood's concept of it than to reality. There were even reindeer sleighs. The fact that there were no reindeer in the Tyrol hardly seemed to matter. The newspaper added: 'A fleet of well-upholstered buses will be waiting to take America's tired millionaires to the foot of the ski slopes. To save them unnecessary exertion three ski-lifts will carry them up to the summits in suspended armchairs.'

The first chair lift was invented by Jim Curran, an American engineer who thought of the idea while working with devices designed to load bananas on to ships. Effectively, Curran decided that skiers were intrinsically no different from bunches of bananas.

Although it is a remote resort, those who love it will travel from almost the ends of the earth to get there – certainly from as far afield as California! Brooke Shields and Margaux Hemingway are

Many think Sun Valley is still the best resort in the States.

among its most loyal devotees – but then they were born there.

Hemingway, of course, is inextricably linked with the history of Sun Valley. By 1939, the resort was paying all Hemingway's expenses to holiday there in return for being allowed to use his name in their advertising material. However, Hemingway only actually skied in Sun Valley once. He preferred to visit the resort for the hunting in the Fall. The great American novelist settled in the small village of Ketchum nearby, and it was here that he eventually took his own life.

Built around the superb Baldy Mountain (for strong skiers) and Dollar (for debutants), Sun Valley opened in 1936 and became famous around the world. But with the advent of jet travel, and the decline of the American railroad system, the ski resort went off the boil too, especially during the emergence in the fifties and sixties of other major new ski resorts. But although the sun sank over the resort, it never quite set and eventually Sun Valley was bought and re-energized by a former downhill ski racer, Bill Janss. Now it is once again being referred to as the 'most pampered mountain in North America.'

New villages of condominiums such as Warm Springs and Elkhorn sprang up. And recently much of the equipment has been updated, with three high-speed detachable 'quad' chairs installed in 1988. They travel at around 1,000 feet per minute – about twice as fast as conventional chairs. Challenger, said to be the largest vertical ski lift in North America, speeds from the bottom of Warm Springs to the top of Baldy in less than ten minutes. Greyhawk services the bottom two-thirds of Warm Springs (1,488 feet), reaching the top in under five minutes. And the new Christmas lift rises from the Roundhouse Restaurant to the top of Baldy Mountain (9,150 feet) in even less time. There is also snow-making equipment available right up to the summit.

But in spite of all these changes – inevitable in order to keep up with the more modern, brasher generation of resorts – that special old-world Sun Valley magic lingers on.

Altogether Sun Valley has more than seventy runs served by almost twenty lifts. Forty-five per cent of the skiing is said to be suitable for intermediates, with seventeen per cent designated 'expert' terrain. Around thirty-eight per cent is suitable for beginners. The longest run is three miles, and snow-making equipment covers well over 250 acres.

A less arduous way of soaking up the atmosphere.

Although the mountains are less dramatic than Wyoming's Tetons or Utah's Wasatch range, they do have a considerable vertical drop of 3,400 feet and include a number of non-stop descents.

When people in Europe are asked to name the best ski resort, some have been known to answer: 'Go to Val d'Isère for a week, then send your skis home and spend another week in Kitzbühel.' The equivalent in America could be: ski in Jackson Hole for a week and then spend a week in Sun Valley. Not that there is anything wrong with the skiing in Kitzbühel or Sun Valley, but in these resorts you can have as much fun not skiing as skiing.

Sun Valley, you might well feel, was built as much with style in mind as substance. For a start, it only enjoys a mere two hundred inches of snow a year, which is not significant when measured against the likes of Snowbird, Alta, Jackson and the rest. But back in the days when Harriman founded the resort, he was not particularly concerned with meteorological charts and jet stream patterns. He was much more interested in attracting the celebrity jet stream – people with names such as Gable, Monroe, Cooper, Crosby and Garland.

Such celebrities would not normally have considered southern Idaho's Sawtooth Mountains to be on their itinerary, so Harriman decided to add a little extra lustre to his beloved resort. He introduced casinos (now outlawed in Idaho) orchestras, heated swimming pools and sumptuous dining facilities at the Sun Valley Lodge. Sun Valley attracted the jet set before the jet had even been invented. There was even a film called *Sun Valley Serenade*, which featured Sonja Henie and the music of Glen Miller. This classic forties romance is screened three times a week. Admission is free.

And if Harriman did not take snow into too much consideration, he was lucky with the sun – or perhaps he did give this aspect more thought, bearing in mind the resort's name. With slopes on three sides of the mountain, you can follow the sun all day. Hence you can start the day riding the lower River Run lift and then make your way to Seattle Ridge and the bowl areas where glorious morning sunshine can make conditions ten degrees warmer than on the Warm Springs side of the mountain.

When there is fresh snow in Sun Valley, the locals make for the bowls. Such swooping descents as Lookout, Little Easter and Mayday receive the immediate and urgent attention of the experts, while intermediates get their excitement from such descents as Siggi's or Far Out. It used to take a considerable time to 'ski out' these areas, but with the advent of the Christmas quad chair, they can be skied with almost indecent haste. Following the sun round, Canyon and Blue Grouse provide useful rehearsals for Sun Valley's *tour de force* mogul run, Exhibition.

The Warm Springs face should by now have lived up to its name as you streak down to Mid Greyhawk and Lower Greyhawk. As Sun Valley's sun fades into the distance, you realize that you are somewhere very special.

When Judy Garland, one of the resort's regular visitors, sang *Somewhere Over The Rainbow*, she might just have had Sun Valley in mind.

SKI FACTS

TRAILS	70
EASIEST	38%
MORE DIFFICULT	45%
MOST DIFFICULT	17%
PEAK ELEVATION	9,150 ft
VERTICAL DROP	3,400 ft
LONGEST RUN	3 miles
CHAIR LIFTS	16 (3 quads, 7 triples and 6 doubles)
AVERAGE SNOWFALL	200 in

TAOS

Taos, a lone, high beacon in the wilds of New Mexico, surrounded by the Carson National Forest and spectacular Sangre de Cristo peaks, with fearsome and steep slopes, bowls, chutes and moguls, 'like Volkswagens half buried in the snow', is a spiritual and physical Shangri-La to cult skiers.

To the west, the high desert plain is suddenly gashed by the Rio Grande Gorge. The local Rocky Mountain peaks – Taos Mountain itself, Wheeler Peak and the three Truchas peaks – rise sharply in the north and east.

The village of Taos dates back almost a thousand years. It was inhabited as long ago as the eleventh century. Even its name has romantic origins. It is the Hispanicized version of a Tiwa phrase (the

Taos – a spiritual and physical Shangri-La to cult skiers.

language spoken by Taos Indians) meaning 'place of the red willows.' The resort has a mysterious and almost mystical atmosphere quite unlike any other ski resort in the USA.

As far as the skiing is concerned, it is sometimes said that Texans turning up at the mock-Alpine ski village for their first visit take one awe-inspired look at the seemingly almost vertical Al's Run – packed with moguls – and with a screeching of tyres perform a U-turn in the parking lot and make a hasty exit for home without so much as slowing down.

For this reason, the legendary owner, Ernie Blake – who, sadly, died in the winter of 1988/89 – erected a sign which reads: 'Don't panic. From this point you can see only one 30th of Taos Ski Valley', advising faint-hearted clients that there are lots of easier slopes higher up.

These include Whitefeather (a name slightly unfairly linked of course with cowardice in battle) and Bambi. A sign also reassures visitors that they do not have to ski Al's if it does not appeal to them. (Another sign informs visitors, Berlin-style, that they are 'leaving the American sector.')

The Taos Ski Valley actually has slopes for every standard, from absolute beginners to the criminally intrepid. Honeysuckle, for example, is a pleasant blue (roughly the American equivalent of a red). Not only is it a link between the front and back of the mountain, but it is an enjoyable warm-up run, so it is skied early in the day by most grades of skier.

Honeysuckle is also the starting point for the somewhat fearsome Walkyries Chute (Götterdämmerung, or Twilight of the Gods, might have been a more appropriate Wagnerian analogy) which is one of the most spectacular runs in Taos.

Off to the right of the benign Bambi run explodes a descent quaintly called Sir Arnold Lunn, which starts out rather alarmingly as a double black diamond (blacker than black, denoted by yellow on American trail maps) but calms down slightly to become 'just' an ordinary black run.

Taos mixes the best of European and American ski traditions in a state that is better known for literature, art and rustic crafts. Taos is rich in folk-lore, Indian culture and D H Lawrence connections.

The British author spent much of his time on a local ranch between 1922 and 1925. He found that the isolation helped him concentrate on his writing.

The ranch was a gift to his wife, Frieda, from the art patron Mabel Dodge Luhan, who was later presented with his manuscript of *Sons and Lovers* in return. Some of Lawrence's controversial paintings can still be viewed at the La Fonda Hotel. Lawrence's shrine is even mentioned as a landmark by the official vacation guide produced by Taos Ski Valley, The Chamber of Commerce and American Express: 'Heading South from Questa on NM3' it says, 'you'll pass the D H Lawrence ranch and shrine, where the famous writer's ashes are kept.'

Lawrence, inspired by the heady cultural cocktail of Taos's legendary Indians, *conquistadors*, mountain men, fur traders, and miners wrote of his time there: 'It was the greatest experience from the outside world that I ever had. It certainly changed me for ever.'

The Indians today are treated with a good deal more respect than they once were. When visiting their adobe, straw and wood apartments in the present-day Pueblo, where some 1,500 of them still live, tourists are asked: 'Remember not to take pictures without first asking permission. The Pueblo is their home, so be considerate in your explorations.'

Lawrence did not have a monopoly on extolling the virtues of Taos. Zane Grey was another writer moved to comment in print. 'You must see, feel, hear and taste this wonderful country' he wrote. 'Once having done so, you will never be the same again.'

As you eventually pass through the small town of Taos itself – with its famous art galleries by the score and its craft shops – and head for the skiing, the road runs through flat desert scrub, sparsely inhabited by the poor peasant farmers depicted in Robert Redford's film *The Milagro Beanfield War*. John Nichols, a local resident who wrote the novel on which the film was based, re-christened the area The Miracle Ski Valley – and aficionados of this skiing area would say the skiing in real life is little short of miraculous.

Ernie Blake, the German-born Swiss who started the resort in 1955, and ran it until his recent death, once had the place virtually to himself. He used to hike out here in the wilds with his family and

friends and ski the area when there was not a single ski lift within hundreds of miles.

In 1937 he had chased his American wife-to-be from Switzerland to Santa Fe. Three years later he promised himself he would live in New Mexico if he survived the Second World War. In 1945, discovering to his satisfaction that he had, he kept his promise. Blake, who lived until his late seventies, was a man who normally got what he wanted.

What he wanted more than anything else was his own ski resort in New Mexico. And he built it in the pine forests twenty miles outside Taos. Remarkably, the latitude is the same as North Africa and Crete, but the desert climate and altitude (the ski resort is at 9,207 feet, and the skiing goes as high as 11,819 feet) conspire to produce freezing nights and snow that is both light and crisp. By day the sunshine is blinding, and to ski without sun cream is a risky business. For those lucky enough to spend entire winters in these exceptionally clear conditions, skin cancer is unfortunately something of an occupational hazard.

Blake, employed at the time by a Texan million- aire who owned the Glenwood Springs resort near Aspen, spotted his beloved north-facing mountain not far from the old mining town of Twining when he was criss-crossing the region in an aircraft while commuting between New Mexico and Colorado. He walked in on skis in three and a half feet of snow for a closer inspection and found that it was good. Exceedingly good.

In the beginning, after installing the first snow- cat and the first T-bar, he and his wife gave lessons and ran the only available accommodation, Hondo Lodge. Today the resort has almost a thousand beds in hotels and condominiums, with a further three thousand available in Taos itself.

Those who are fortunate enough to stay in the ski resort are able to walk straight from the compact, low-rise European-style village on to nursery slopes or chose from six chair lifts which provide access to the main skiing areas. The intermediate network centres on the Kachina lift, which also takes skiers to one of Taos's two mountain restaurants and to the coin-operated giant slalom courses.

Taos, which is steeped in Indian culture, is a fascinating resort which intrigued D H Lawrence. It inspired his writing and his painting.

But there is little doubt that it is the advanced skier who will enjoy Taos most. Al's Run, which goes straight down under the main chair lift, is challenging enough, and to make matters worse, everyone riding up can contemplate the fate of those who lose their battle with gravity in the most spectacular style on the way down.

Like Al's, other so-called 'ego-busters' such as Snakedance, Longhorn and Inferno are never groomed. Real experts and other skiers determined to risk inflicting serious damage to their limbs, head straight for the 'double-diamond' (extra black) chutes leading off the High Traverse.

A popular habit for a group skiing together is to take it in turn to set off in front of the rest of the party and pick a descent of his or her choice. Those anxious to lose friends should go for Thunderbird, Oster, Fabian or Stauffenberg (a narrow, steep chute reached only after a heart-stopping traverse above even narrower chutes). No wonder Taos describes its skiing in such ambivalent terms as 'Awesome and Inviting terrain.'

Taos takes particular pride in its ski school. Ernie Blake, who ran it until his death, used to say mischievously: 'It *is* possible to learn to ski in Taos without instruction. After all, the Wright brothers learned to fly without instruction. The thing to consider is that the survival rate is low!'

The most accessible off-piste skiing is in the chutes off the Highline and Tresckow Ridges, a twenty-minute walk from the top of Chair Lift Two. Those sufficiently energetic to climb for a further hour or so can ski down from Kachina peak. A guide is recommended for these descents, although not essential. However, skiers are forbidden to tackle them alone and all those who wish to go must notify the ski patrol at the top of Chair Lift Two before noon.

The vertical drop at Taos is a healthy 2,612 feet, with just over half the seventy-two runs in the 'expert' category. The remaining half is divided almost exactly between intermediate and beginner levels.

The mountains act as a trap for western storms, and clouds soak up moisture over the Sea of Cortez and then dry out as they pass over the desert. The result, as Blake described it, is 'powder that is fluffy as egg whites and dependable as a Swiss watch.' The average annual snowfall is 323 inches.

Had Blake built a lift up to Kachina Ridge, he would have achieved a vertical drop of 3,000 feet. But he did not want to. 'Americans are too lazy', he was fond of saying. 'The hike is good for them.'

Christmas is an especially magical time to visit Taos. One of the local customs is to fill porrones – hand-blown Mexican glass flasks – with Martinis, bury them in the snow and send skiers out in search of them. Another is to decorate the adobe buildings of the town of Taos with farolitos – festive lights made from candles in paper bags filled with sand. The Pueblo Indians light bonfires of pinon trees which burn red and orange, and dancers in masks carrying flaming corn husks form torchlight processions.

One thing is certain: whenever they arrive, skiers of any category will find Taos one of the most fascinating locations in the world, never mind the astonishing skiing. Put the two together, and you get something approaching a mystical experience.

SKI FACTS

TRAILS	72
EASIEST	24%
MORE DIFFICULT	25%
MOST DIFFICULT	51%
PEAK ELEVATION	11,819 ft
VERTICAL DROP	2,612 ft
CHAIR LIFTS	7 (1 triple and 6 doubles)
TOWS	2
AVERAGE SNOWFALL	323 in

TELLURIDE

Some people suggest that Telluride is named after tellurium, a gold-bearing ore found in the San Juan mountains. Others claim that it means 'to hell you ride', an allusion to the boisterous gaming parlours and infamous brothels in the so-called 'Popcorn Alley' of the old mining town back in the 1880s. It is such a stunningly beautiful place that I prefer to believe it was connected with natural metals rather than human debauchery. Few people who gaze on its awe-inspiring beauty are unmoved. In 1903, T A Rickard wrote in his *Across the San Juan Mountains*:

The Indians called it sacred. Now the white man reveres the snow.

The grim desolation of time-worn summits and crumbling crags reached down into the gloomy gorge of the San Miguel, which suddenly broadened into the sunlit valley of Telluride, checkered with cultivation and bright with the gleam of blue water. Beyond were green foothills, out of which arose the sculptured mass of Mt Wilson, silhouetted against the setting sun, and further still, northwestward, rim upon rim of far-off hills fading into the bourne of distant Utah.

Eighty six years later, writers who now have the benefit of flight to add to the wonder of it all, are still mesmerized by the landscape. Rob Schultheis talks of 'roaming the skies between Lizard Head, Upper Tomboy and Horsefly Mesa.' In the Telluride magazine he continues:

The country unfolded below us like the most complex origami sculpture in the world, revealing infinite convolutions of timber, meadows, avalanche chutes, snowfields and streams, along with the frail constructions of man: abandoned farmsteads, isolated cabins and dusty roads coiling up into high wild valleys.

There are also huge frozen waterfalls such as Cornet Creek Falls which are actually climbed in spectacular style by local mountain guides.

Telluride, like the best (but not necessarily the biggest) of the gold-nuggets that used to be mined in its once busy gold-mine areas is waiting to be discovered. It has been earmarked for some years as 'an awakening giant.' And I suspect that this fascinating town in a spectacular wilderness is about to burst into the skiing world's consciousness like a newly discovered comet. It certainly deserves to. But some people who feel protective about Telluride hope it does not.

A newly constructed airport just outside the town may make it happen – hopefully not at the expense of the wild, isolated, magical atmosphere that Telluride has clung on to for so many years. However, since it is part of a protected National Historic District, it is to be hoped that any explosion in skiing popularity will not spoil its unique charm.

Everywhere I travel in the American West, people are singing its praises. Telluride – in a fairly remote part of south-west Colorado not too far from New Mexico – is a little like a smaller but sometimes steeper version of the fabulous Jackson Hole ski resort. It is hidden away in the Uncompahgre National Forest at the end of an eighteen-mile box canyon formed by the San Miguel river, dominated on three sides by really spectacular 14,000-foot peaks. Visually, the impact is stunning and unmatched by any other Colorado resort.

There is a feeling here that life has been stripped of all its veneers. You feel so close to the land that you can almost feel the earth breathe and the shrubs grow. After a while, you start to hear things in the woods that you have never heard before – like the faint echo of a coyote in the wind or an elk stepping nimbly through the forest. Much of the unique flavour of the old West has been lost – or never been discovered – in most ski resorts in America. Telluride is one of the few exceptions. The denim-and-dirt village is one of the few tangible remnants of the way the West once was.

Although cowboys no longer walk the streets with six-shooters tied to their hips or spurs jangling on their boots, they do still wear wide-brimmed hats and they do sometimes have leathery hands and faces from herding cattle or hauling hay (instead of merely posing for ski resort promotional photographs as they do in some resorts).

But if one of these cowboys takes his hat off, the chances are that a long lock of shoulder-length hair might come cascading out. In the sixties places like Telluride – in a dead-end, out-of-the-way canyon on the road to nowhere – attracted a number of hippies who eventually found a niche for themselves on the range or in the hills.

During the height of Colorado's gold rush, Telluride boasted a population of 5,000 who could chose from fifty bars, gaming houses and bordellos.

It was from here that the legendary Butch Cassidy made, as the Americans put it, his 'first unauthorized bank withdrawal.' He and his 'wild bunch' robbed the San Miguel Valley Bank in 1889. Inevitably, the Cassidy connection is reflected in present-day Telluride. There is a Cassidy's restaurant at the base of Coonskin.

As in Park City and Breckenridge, the city fathers of the old town have carefully preserved and restored many of its original and charming Victorian wood and brick buildings, and Main Street is a showpiece.

For the Ute Indians, the valley was sacred. They called its peaks 'the shining mountains' and refused white men access through the canyon 'doors.' But the miners, spurred on by thoughts of gold, silver and copper, trecked over the top of 13,000-foot peaks from the east with mule trains, and those who survived were often richly rewarded for their efforts.

By 1890, Telluride had mushroomed from a collection of tents and cabins to a town with a population of 3,000. A year later, the Rio Grande railroad reached town. Colorado Avenue was lined with shops, livery stables, saloons and gambling halls. Like Aspen, Telluride suffered badly from the 'silver crash' of 1893 when the silver standard was abolished. But this was followed by a gold boom. The New Sheridan Hotel, the 'pride of Telluride' was built in 1895 and celebrities who later stayed there included Lillian Gish and Sarah Bernhardt. The Continental Room (now Julian's Restaurant) had sixteen booths with velvet curtains equipped with telephones so that diners who

wished for privacy could order their meals without being disturbed by hovering waiters. Male chauvinism was obviously flourishing: women were required to enter the side-door in order to 'wait the gentleman's pleasure to dine.' The old saloon (now the Sheridan Bar) still has calfskin-covered walls and a bar made from cherry wood imported from Austria.

Further down Main Street, the Roma Bar – once one of the oldest and wildest saloons – still contains its valuable 1860 bar of carved walnut with its exquisite twelve-foot French mirrors.

Another building with an intriguing history is Waterfall House, a survivor of a spectacular cloudburst in 1914 when Cornet Creek sent a torrent of mud and rocks through the town depositing five feet of debris from the Liberty Bell mine down to Colorado Avenue. One woman was killed and the Sheridan was filled with mud half way to the ceiling.

And L L Nunn's house is a reminder of the production of the first high-voltage alternating current power plant in the world. Nunn sent his current to the Gold King Mine a few miles away,

The magic of Telluride and its fabulous mountains lit by moonlight.

and from then on miners no longer had to rely on coal or timber for their power. By 1894 most of the mines and the entire town were lit by electricity.

By the turn of the century the gold rush too was fading and by 1930 the Bank of Telluride had closed and the population had dwindled to 512 (which at least was 505 more than Breckenridge!). The bank's president, Charles Waggoner, was jailed after ensuring that the people of Telluride got their money – at the expense of the New York banks. 'I would rather see the New York banks lose money' he told the court, 'than the people of Telluride, most of whom have worked all their lives for the savings that were deposited in my bank.'

Just as miners were once richly rewarded, it was soon to become the turn of skiers. In 1945, a rope tow was installed in Town Park. It only lasted two years, but in 1958 it was reconstructed – powered this time by an old automobile motor. A season's lift pass during that first year was $5. Sixty locals bought one.

Ten years later, with Telluride boarded up and virtually a ghost town, a Beverly Hills entrepreneur, Joe Zoline, arrived with plans to build a 'winter recreation area second to none.' By 1971, Telluride had become a boom town again. This time it was caused by skiing. The skiing is certainly dramatic although not on quite the same scale as that of Jackson. But it does have some of the longest, steepest bump runs in Colorado.

The most significant change in the skiing here came in 1986 when – in spite of strong resistance from the local people who feared that their quaint resort was going to be 'Aspenized' – two lifts were built which dramatically changed the overall uphill transport facilities. The new Sunshine Express is claimed to be the longest high-speed chair lift in the world.

Such runs as True, The Plunge (reputedly the longest, steepest run in Colorado) and Spiral Stairs, which would test any skier with their severe moguls and fearsome fall-lines, have suddenly become much easier to reach. Previously, you had to drive for about twenty minutes around the mountain to get to the main lifts.

The other two faces, the Gorrono and Sunshine, are less severe and are therefore popular with intermediate skiers.

The vertical drop, which can take you over knee-buckling moguls that are sometimes as big as lorries, is more than three thousand feet and the snow record varies between two hundred and four hundred inches, often including some excellent powder. In spite of its Jackson-like machismo image, Telluride has -- according to the American *Skiing Magazine* – one of the best beginners' areas in the US in the Prospect Meadows region.

Telluride is ripe for development. It seems inevitable. For some, the best is yet to come. All the more reason to visit it as soon as you can and not wait for the condominiums, at present on the drawing-board, to spring up. Telluride is still something right out of the 'Old West'. It may not be for too much longer.

SKI FACTS

TRAILS	46
EASIEST	24%
MORE DIFFICULT	50%
MOST DIFFICULT	26%
PEAK ELEVATION	12,247 ft
VERTICAL DROP	3,155 ft
CHAIR LIFTS	9 (1 quad, 2 triples and 6 doubles)
TOWS	1
AVERAGE SNOWFALL	300 in

TELLURIDE

VAIL

For centuries, the only form of life that left its footprints in the deep snows of Vail Valley were grizzly bears, mountain lions and bighorn sheep wintering in the caves and rocky ledges. Even the Ute Indians left the valley when the snows came.

Those peaceful but desolate days are long gone. Today the valley in winter is swarming with skiers from every corner of the globe. Vail has become one of the world's greatest ski resorts – some would argue the greatest.

This ultimate in ski paradises has been given a tremendously unfair advantage – its natural bowls. It is as if some almighty force – during the creation of the Americas – was dispensing a bowl each to skiing areas that would be built millions of years in the future. But for some reason this force became careless and dropped a whole stack of bowls – 2,500 acres worth – on one Colorado mountain like a clumsy waiter dropping soup bowls. Except that this 'clumsiness' turned out to be a godsend. The result is Game Creek Bowl, Sun Up Bowl, Sun Down Bowl, Tea Cup Bowl, China Bowl, Siberia Bowl and Mongolia Bowl.

Until the winter of 1988/89 China Bowl was only available to skiers taking special snow-cat tours. Now, as part of a $15 million expansion programme instigated by Vail's new owner George

Vail's magical skiing terrain can be likened to a huge patchwork quilt of trails.

skiing, hardpack, corn snow in the spring, or at worst, less pleasant snow conditions of various types such as breakable crust, sun crust or wind-packed snow. The point is that the snow is left alone for those who want to ski the best, and if necessary the worst – the whole snow spectrum – rather than have it all blandly prepared for them by a machine.

Vail has also just added a second detachable 'quad', the Born Free Express at Lions Head. And at Game Creek Bowl, an upgraded quad plus a number of new runs have added an enormous amount of variety to the skiing.

If you asked a computer to design the best ski resort in the world, with the emphasis both on variety and the best possible bowl skiing it would be hard-pressed to improve on Vail, the only real pedestrian ski town in America. It is known as the 'something for everyone' resort, and any skier of any ability could not fail to be happy there whether for just an hour or a whole month of Ski-Sundays.

It is huge, and its runs are tremendously varied, flawlessly organized and beautifully groomed. With its sister resort Beaver Creek nine miles down the road it can employ as many as six hundred instructors at peak times.

Finding even a hint of an Achilles' heel at Vail is a daunting task. If it has one at all, it may be that the skiing and the resort itself is just the tiniest bit bland. What it lacks, possibly, is just a little of the swashbuckling excitement of Jackson Hole. Cliffs, rocks and chutes are a little on the scarce side in Vail, but it has an abundance of everything else, especially that wonderful back-bowl skiing for which it is so deservedly famous. One run – in Sun Down Bowl - had the rare distinction of virtually christening itself. It is called Wow! – an almost involuntary gasp you give as the run, already quite steep, suddenly falls away into an unexpectedly even steeper section leaving your stomach skiing a foot or two above your head. Who knows, perhaps the first person to try it said something even more expressive than Wow! But then you probably could not print *that* on a trail map!

Gillett (who bought Vail and Beaver Creek for $130 million in 1985) a new quadruple chair, the Orient Express, has opened up the bowl to other skiers. They can now ski to Tea Cup, then on to Siberia – or take another new lift to Mongolia Bowl.

Now that China and Siberia Bowls have been put 'on the trail map' Vail's official ski terrain has more than doubled – an extraordinary development considering that Vail was already America's largest single mountain resort.

The bowls are where you help yourself to Vail's fabulous powder. They are left ungroomed, so that even when the powder is skied out, skiers can still enjoy natural snow conditions, be it deep snow

Vail, almost exactly one hundred miles from Denver, was built quite recently – in 1962. 'One day' says a guide-book to the area, 'it was a sheep mountain. The next it was an "internationally famous" ski resort!' But its origins were less recent that this might suggest.

The men who built Vail had first absorbed the atmosphere of the neighbourhood as long ago as 1942, when the US Army opened Camp Hale on Tennessee Pass, twenty miles south-west of the valley. The 10th Mountain Division – the only US Mountain Troups to see action in the Second World War – trained here (and at Aspen). Among them was Pete Seibert, who later founded the ski resort, and Bob Parker and Bill 'Sarge' Brown, who helped him.

But even they had not explored the valley itself or realized its potential. The best slopes were hidden from view above the highway. It was Earl Eaton, who was prospecting for uranium who 'stumbled' on Vail Mountain and realized he had struck something more precious. He was a friend of Seibert's. Together they hiked to the summit of the mountain and when they saw the enormous potential, they were immediately determined to develop it as a ski area.

Rightly or wrongly the designers tried to make the centre look like their idea of an Austro/Swiss mountain village. This works reasonably well in that it does, superficially at least, capture a little of the flavour of a traditional Alpine resort. However there are those who like to mock, and refer to Vail as a 'plastic Bavaria.' In a sense it is all just a shade ersatz. But the skiing certainly is not.

There are more than one hundred marked trails of every conceivable description, plus one or two inconceivable ones. Unlike its rival, Aspen, a third of Vail's main ski area is suitable for beginners.

It really is a 'something for everyone' mountain, and children are especially well catered for. Rather than listen to their parents' exploits at the end of the day, the children can make their *parents* envious with tales of derring-do on their own special

Vail is characterized by its chic, 'European' style.

children-orientated trails. With Beaver Creek, Vail has, under Gillett, taken pains to specialize in children's theme runs. There are roller-coaster bump rides called Whoopedee-doos and Wiggly-Waglees. Plus special features such as a 'Hibernating' Bear and a 'Mountain Lion' in caves that children can ski through, and other attractions like Dragon's Breath Mine, Monstrous Mounds and Fort Whippersnapper. There is even a special trail map for children which 'translates' many of the runs into their 'language' from the less imaginative adult version. Here children no longer feel like mere appendages of their parents. They even have their own personal ski instructor, Captain Zembo. A delightful chap called John Alderson was playing this role during my last visit to Beaver Creek.

During Vail's first winter, an extraordinary thing happened. There was a shortage of snow. The Southern Ute tribal dancers were called in to perform a snow dance. To everyone's surprise it worked. Eighteeen inches of snow fell within twenty-four hours.

At 8,200 feet, with skiing as high as 11,250 feet, Vail rarely has problems with insufficient snow. However, just to be on the safe side, like most American ski resorts, Vail has brought in snow-making equipment. This covers more than 320 acres at key points on the mountain. But natural snow accounts for a healthy 325 inches a year.

Ironically, it was the Ute Indians – later so obliging with their snow dance – who in earlier times had a lot to do with some of Vail's widest trails. They created huge clearings in the forest with what became known as 'grudge' fires. When the first white men came to the area – hunters and trappers, followed by miners and lumberjacks – the Utes were so angry that they set fire to large areas of the forest to try to prevent the white man from capitalizing on their lands. Many of these fires opened up some of the wide-open slopes that are so characteristic of such Colorado resorts as Vail, Aspen, Copper Mountain and Breckenridge.

In spite of my bias for Jackson Hole, I have to admit that Vail, in terms of across-the-spectrum skiing for all classes of skier, is probably the closest to being the world's perfect ski resort. Just as the Matterhorn is probably more beautiful and accessible than a mountain like K2.

SKI FACTS

	VAIL
TRAILS	100+ (3,787 acres)
EASIEST	32%
MORE DIFFICULT	36%
MOST DIFFICULT	32%
PEAK ELEVATION	11,350 ft
VERTICAL DROP	3,200 ft
GONDOLAS	1 6-passenger
CHAIR LIFTS	19 (7 quads, 3 triples and 9 doubles)
TOWS	2
AVERAGE SNOWFALL	325 in
	BEAVER CREEK
TRAILS	800 acres
EASIEST	23%
MORE DIFFICULT	43%
MOST DIFFICULT	34%
PEAK ELEVATION	11,440 ft
VERTICAL DROP	3,340 ft
CHAIR LIFTS	9 (1 quad, 5 triples and 3 doubles)

BANFF/ LAKE LOUISE

Nature has been kind to Lake Louise and its surrounding satellite ski resorts. The craggy peaks rise above expansive forests of first-generation spruce which are so thick that from the air or from the highest slopes they almost resemble the jungles of South America. And there can be few places where you can walk down the main street and encounter a herd of elk with thighs like oak trees crossing your path!

There are three major ski areas in the Rocky Mountain region that straddles the border between British Columbia and Alberta. Sunshine Village, Mount Norquay and arguably the finest – the Banff/Lake Louise complex, the largest ski resort in Canada.

It is a magical place, with hot springs hub-bubbling up through granite rocks, cross-country trails meandering through forests and past glacial lakes, and encounters (not too close) with bighorn sheep as well as elk.

The town of Banff itself is in Banff National Park – Canada's oldest park, which covers 2,564 square miles. It is a picturesque place nestling among sky-scraping mountains. There is nothing else quite like it in North America. For some people, like the actor William Shatner who boldly goes there regularly, it is the best. 'It's so beautiful' he told me when we met in Los Angeles. 'It's my favourite ski resort.'

Mount Norquay, a relatively small ski area ten minutes away from the town, is popular with local skiers.

Norquay, which overlooks the town of Banff and the Bow Valley has two major attractions for local inhabitants. it is nearby and it is steep. But although The Face or Lone Pine runs are certainly imposing – and come alarmingly close to straining your neck as you gaze up at them – there is a more than adequate terrain suitable for beginners off to the side of the steep Face.

From the top of the Norquay Double Chair to the Day Lodge at the bottom skiers can accomplish 1,300 feet of vertical drop. This may be small by some standards, but skiers with a quest for steeper, longer runs have other options.

The North American slope, which starts at the top of Norquay Chair winds its way down to the foot of the town of Banff. A great final run (or one to be enjoyed just before lunch) the descent drops 2,450 vertical feet.

By moving fifteen miles down the Trans-Canadian Highway and then down a four-mile access road, you arrive at the resort of Sunshine – so called because it is perched in a wide aperture between the surrounding peaks. To reach the actual ski slopes, you must take a four-mile gondola ride. High on a meadow basin is a cluster of buildings constructed in log-cabin style, plus a modern lodge and four lifts that radiate in different directions.

Its elevation (6,200 feet) assures the healthiest snowfall of Banff's three ski areas. Although the name Sunshine does not exactly leap from the tongues of North American powder hounds, it does have as much snow as any other resort in Canada, with around four hundred inches a year.

Although Sunshine advertises a 3,497-foot vertical drop, this is only truly accomplished during the last run of the day (or the last run before lunch, perhaps) down to the parking lot. Most skiers do not spend time completing the final section of this run, so in realistic terms the vertical drop is more like 2,000 feet.

So far north that even south-facing slopes don't lose their sparkle.

Banff: gateway to the Canadian Rockies.

Nonetheless, there is plenty of good skiing at an altitude that is immune to the freak Chinook winds which arrive in February bringing warm air from the south-western United States.

Sunshine was part of the World Cup circuit in 1984. For intermediates and families searching for a mountain where you can spread out but not lose each other, Sunshine is ideal.

Thus members of the same group could ski trails such as Spring Hill, Highway One or Bye Bye Bowl on the Angel and Great Divide lifts over and over again without really parting company.

For the more adventurous, especially when there is fresh snow, the trails off the Teepee Town Chair make a good foray.

But to ski only Norquay or Sunshine would probably leave most skiers hungry for more, and it is probably fair to say that you should ski both resorts and Lake Louise itself in order to be able to leave replete. The resort of Louise is 'only' another thirty miles down the road (to the Canadians anything less than a hundred miles is merely down the road).

Banff/Lake Louise, with two triple chairs and four doubles, has wide-open bowls above the tree-line and trails cut through the forest which will keep any skier busy for a week or more. The ski area is divided into three zones: South Face, Back Bowls and the Larch area.

You can reach the top of its 3,250-foot vertical drop simply by riding the Olympic Chair and the Summit T-Bar, two of the four uphill transport systems on the South Face. These are the busiest of Lake Louise's slopes and the site of an accredited World Cup downhill and giant slalom course.

Few resort developers would dream of locating ski slopes on a mountain with a southern exposure, but at Lake Louise – where the Arctic air current does not have far to travel to cause a strong effect – the designers got away with establishing primary runs in an area which in more southerly resorts would be asking for trouble.

The exposure on the back bowls, where skiing is above the tree-line, is entirely north facing. Thus the powder remains well preserved days after it has fallen. Access to the back bowls is via the East Chair or the Summit T-Bar. The majority of runs are graded 'expert' but there are several trails for beginners and intermediates.

From the bowl area, the Paradise Chair climbs back to an elevation from which two runs on either side of the South Face are available. But before you return to the South Face, the most popular area on the mountain, it would be an opportune moment to ski the Larch area. From here the Ski Out trail – a four-mile run for beginners – brings you back to the South Face.

Banff/Lake Louise is a vast, beautiful skiing area with as much skiing as Vail, even if you include the Colorado resort's newly opened Back Bowls, China and Siberia. The resort also has the most spectacular scenery.

The skiing is a good mix. Intermediates especially will enjoy this resort. Forty per cent of the skiing is designated for them. Twenty five per cent of the mountain is considered to be suitable for beginners, and the remaining thirty-five per cent is for experts.

Although Banff/Lake Louise has taken the precaution of installing what are claimed to be the most extensive snow-making facilities in western Canada, it is sufficiently far north for the skiing here to be a really cold experience. But no matter where you might find yourself in this chain of resorts, there will be a warm waiting area within reach. And you should not have to search far to find a hot meal readily at hand. In such below-zero temperatures, one bite will delight!

Three day lodges: Whiskeyjack at the base, the Temple on the back side or the Whitehorn on the eastern fringe of the South Face offer good food and – just as important – a warm fire.

Banff/Lake Louise also has some unusually fine hotels. Perhaps none captures the interest of visitors more than the Banff Springs Hotel. Built more than fifty years ago, it resembles a huge castle in the mountains. Equally elegant is the Lake Louise Chateau situated in a positively majestic position at the foot of Lake Louise.

Considering that as Captain Kirk, William Shatner had the entire universe to choose from, he did not make a bad choice when he started coming to Banff and Lake Louise. And kept coming.

SKI FACTS

TRAILS	130
EASIEST	25%
MORE DIFFICULT	40%
MOST DIFFICULT	35%
PEAK ELEVATION	8,300 ft
VERTICAL DROP	3,497 ft
CHAIR LIFTS	13 (1 quad, 2 triples and 10 doubles)
TOWS	6
AVERAGE SNOWFALL	400 in

WHISTLER/ BLACKCOMB

Whistler is one of only two resorts in the whole of North America with a vertical drop of more than 5,000 feet. Both in fact are in Canada, and the second, its arch rival Blackcomb is right next door! They share the same lift pass and even the same ski village at Whistler and their base terminals are only yards apart. Yet at present the two are locked into an expensive, possibly healthy but otherwise seemingly pointless battle to install new equipment and persuade the skiing public that each is the better resort.

In 1987/88, Blackcomb installed three high speed 'quad' chairs with pull-down perspex covers to protect skiers from extremes of weather. Whistler countered with a new ten-passenger gondola, the Whistler Express. This transports skiers to the Roundhouse Station in eighteen minutes. It was now Blackcomb's next move.

They have replied with Showcase T-bar, a second 'floating' lift on the ice of Horstman Glacier. This helps Blackcomb's claim to be the 'only ski mountain in North Amercia where you can find year-round glacier skiing.' The lift also opens up a new area for winter skiers. In the summer of 1988 the resort also blasted a connecting platform in the rockfaces that bridge the two massive glaciers of Horstman and Blackcomb. Last winter too five miles of new trails were opened up and the snow-making machinery was dramatically increased.

No doubt we shall hear soon what Whistler comes up with in reply. Vancouver, just seventy miles away, provides most of the skiers who are benefiting from this ambivalent rivalry.

Whistler, the older of the two by twenty years, offers some of the most demanding skiing above the tree-line in North America. But Blackcomb, with its Seventh Heaven Express just steals it on height. At 5,280 feet it is 174 vertical feet higher than Whistler, and thus has the biggest vertical drop in the whole of North America.

However, much depends on how many different lifts it takes to reach the top of a vertical drop, no matter how high. Chamonix, for example, offers one of the biggest vertical drops in Europe, but if it takes half the morning to reach the top of the Vallée Blanche, then you can accomplish as many turns per hour at resorts with a lower vertical but non-stop uphill transport. So when Whistler added its new gondola it improved things dramatically because it covers eighty per cent of its 5,000-odd vertical feet in one journey. Thus what once took forty minutes is now accomplished in sixteen.

What kind of snow you may experience tends to be in the lap of the gods of precipitation. British Columbia can be a little like California in this respect. Because of its proximity to the Pacific – the moss which drapes parts of the conifer forest is a manifestation of this – the snow is often moist, and not always a 'powder-hound's' dream. And with peak elevations of only 8,000 feet, the resorts' lower slopes suffer the vicissitudes of the weather more easily than at higher resorts.

Opened more than a decade ago, Blackcomb – owned partly by the Aspen Ski Corporation – has more than fifty trails, many hugging the fall-line from start to finish. Seven triple chair lifts provide the uphill transportation. Among the most testing runs are Gearjammer, Cruiser and Mainline. In good conditions, dropping 4,000 feet on a well-groomed trail, you sometimes feel that your skis are on automatic pilot.

But although Whistler does not possess the number of 'pure-bred' fall-line trails that Blackcomb enjoys it does have 2,000 acres of skiing that

The twin resorts of Whistler and Blackcomb in Canada – North America's biggest vertical drops.

combines the best of bowl and trail skiing. There is also some excellent helicopter skiing available from Whistler Village using the Western Ice Cap glaciers and Chilcotin mountains.

With the West, Whistler, Harmony and Burnt Stew Bowls, there would be enough terrain on good powder days to keep the entire Royal Canadian Mounted Police Force happy. When January and February bring the coldest weather to the high peaks, there is the greatest chance of powder. Although never in the Utah category of finest, driest and lightest, it can still be vastly enjoyable to ski. There is an amusingly chauvinistic touch at Whistler: Dad's Run (Trail 13) is a black. Mom's Run, running parallel to it, is green. Below the bowls there are descents like Franz's Run, Gondola Run and the World Cup downhill course which rivals almost anything at neighbouring Blackcomb.

But at the end of the day comparisons are probably odious and whether you prefer Whistler or Blackcomb of these two mighty snow-clad peaks is a subjective experience. Better to immerse yourself in the hot tubs at Whistler Springs and give thanks for not one but *two* great resorts.

Whistler village – in both camps.

SKI FACTS

	WHISTLER
TRAILS	96
EASIEST	25%
MORE DIFFICULT	55%
MOST DIFFICULT	20%
PEAK ELEVATION	7,140 ft
VERTICAL DROP	5,106 ft
GONDOLAS	1 10-passenger (Whistler Express) 1 4-passenger
CHAIR LIFTS	10 (3 triples and 7 doubles)
TOWS	5
AVERAGE SNOWFALL	450 in
	BLACKCOMB
TRAILS	85
EASIEST	20%
MORE DIFFICULT	55%
MOST DIFFICULT	25%
PEAK ELEVATION	7,494 ft
VERTICAL DROP	5,280 ft
CHAIR LIFTS	9 (3 quads, 5 triples and 1 double)
TOWS	3

BARILOCHE

Half-way down the vast length of that stunning mountain range, the Andes, tucked beside a great lake in the province of Rio Negro lies San Carlo de Bariloche. Jetting in on the regular Aerolineas Argentinas flight to Bariloche International Airport, you experience a truly magnificent view of the towering spires which give the ski area its name of Gran Catedral.

Founded in the 1890s as a small settlement around a chapel, Bariloche is now a big town with sufficient beds for 20,000 tourists. With some surprise, you find yourself looking at buildings you thought you had left behind in the Northern Hemisphere: chalets!

Like many American towns – North and South – Bariloche has been influenced by groups of Europeans fleeing from oppression in their own

countries. This can produce some quaint cultural oddities. There is more than a whiff of *gemutlichkeit* in Bariloche's wood-carved chalets, many of whose owners still have Austrian or German names. There is also a Danish settlement nearby, and in the streets many blonde Nordic faces mingle with the olive complexions of the Spanish and the swarthy features of the Incas. The people are usually friendly and welcoming, and have the innate pride of the Spaniards. Incidentally, while it may not be advisable to 'mention the war', the natives in general do not seem to bear a grudge about the terrible events of 1982 and are outwardly just as friendly towards the British as anyone else.

Bariloche is an attractive, busy town which curves around one end of the great Lake Nahuel Huapi (pronounced narwal hwapi). It all sounds a

A long schuss by road to the Andes.

Races are held regularly on the mountain and there is a good downhill course approved by the International Ski Federation. The network of groomed trails includes a number of easy greens for beginners. The season can start as early as May and lasts until September.

At the base of the lift system there is some hotel, hostel and club accommodation, but most visitors prefer to stay in Bariloche itself. There are also cafes and restaurants on the slopes – although perhaps not in the same numbers as in Zermatt!

In common with Taos, New Mexico, there is a strong Indian subculture, although the customs are different. Here the Indians still re-enact an intriguing old ritual when cooking. They dig a pit, line it with hot stones, and then cover the whole lot with earth. This is a variant of the 'volcanic' cooking practised in some parts of Iceland and New Zealand. Many hours later, the Indians dig the game up again and eat it. It is delicious. But if you do not particularly relish the idea, you can opt instead for a more straightforward dish called *asado* – a whole sheep barbecued on open fires.

Lake Nahual Huapi and Victoria Island have an unusual claim to fame. The area was used by Walt Disney as the visual back-cloth for his film *Bambi*, although perhaps the idea of a young fawn with frail legs flailing on a frozen lake is not quite the public-relations image that Bariloche would necessarily wish to exploit.

The lake is stocked with salmon and trout and the island teems with game, so Bariloche's summer season is every bit as important as its winter.

Although there are definite similarities between Bariloche, Las Lenas and the other smaller Argentinian ski resorts, there is a very distinctive flavour to skiing in the Andes. It is a great, immense land and you will be sharing the mountain tops with condors rather than Alpine choughs.

When you have finished your visit, the snows of the Northern Hemisphere will be awaiting you . . . unless you care to linger on and sample the delights of a summer on Victoria Island. Bariloche is that kind of place. You may not want to come home in a hurry.

million miles away from St Moritz, but ski towns the world over have similar basic needs. Thus Bariloche has its ski shops, where you can buy or hire equipment, and even the inevitable disco. Local leather goods and woven handicrafts are the specialities of the region and worth bringing home.

The slopes lie some nineteen kilometres (twelve miles) away by road, but there is a regular bus service. Three chair lifts and a dozen tows serve an area which stretches from 955 metres (3,133 feet) to just over 2000 metres (6,512 feet). It can become slushy at the bottom of the ski area, but there is often good powder on top.

The sun can shine here with considerable warmth. It takes a little time to adjust to the idea that in Argentina the north-facing slopes face the sun while those facing south hold the powder!

LAS LENAS

In 1982, I was one of the many journalists who helped to cover the war with Argentina the easy way – by monitoring television news programmes. It never occurred to me that one day I would be writing about the skiing there ... especially a resort that was built *after* the conflict. I was not even certain that one *could* ski there although I knew vaguely that there was skiing somewhere in the Andes, which are, after all, the second highest mountain range in the world.

The first impression of the skiing in Las Lenas – founded in Mendoza province as recently as June 1983 – was that the scenery was not so different from that of the Alps, except that the rocks were often an orangey colour, a little similar to the colours you find in the Italian Dolomites. But although 40,000 trees have been planted around the resort, Las Linas is way above the natural tree-line, so for the time being the similarity ends there.

The resort, naturally, is purpose built, with chalets and apartments looking like triangles and pyramids of wood lying in the snow. It could almost be a section of one of the better known purpose-built French resorts such as Les Arcs or La Plagne. Even the lifts have a familiar look – they were built by the European manufacturers, Poma.

The resort is growing each year: a new telecabine has been constructed for the Pan American Championships, and the resort is host to speed-skiing events and World Cup racing. European teams, including the Swiss and Italians do some of their out-of-season training here because Las Lenas is regarded as one of the best resorts south of the equator.

It is ideal for families, and intermediates, and there is considerable potential for powder skiers. There are six black runs, and every week there is a torchlight descent – also reminiscent of many resorts in the Alps.

You can tell a lot about ski resorts from the type of music they play over their tannoy systems, which can make the atmosphere completely different from resort to resort. In places like Grindelwald, it tends to be oompahs and yodels, which actually

make the skiing jolly and breezy. In Colorado – Aspen, for example – it is much more likely to be 'heavy metal' blasting and echoing around the base of Ajax Mountain, although the Beatles are perhaps the most commonly heard skiing accompaniment in North America. Here in Las Lenas, on the Eros run, however, it was Sinatra.

Jupiter, Apolo, Minerva and Neptuna were next and then it was time for lunch in Bacus, one of the two mountain lodges. This time Dire Straits was on the musical menu and again it could have been just about any mountain restaurant in the Alps.

It was a chance to discuss the war with Roberto Thostrup, an instructor who had spent a number of winters teaching in Europe. The conversation continued after lunch on the chair lift up to the second highest point at 3430 metres (11,250 feet). Thostrup said it had been a 'terrible event' that should never have happened – and it was ridiculous that Britain and Argentina were still technically 'at war.' He said that most people in Argentina felt the same. It was much the same attitude that I had met when I was skiing with an Argentinian in the Spanish resort of Sol y Nieve right in the middle of the Falklands conflict.

But this was six years on, and all thoughts of wars were forgotten at the top station where the true enormity and the sheer brilliance of the Andes were revealed. As far as the eye could see there were jagged, snow-capped peaks. In one direction, the valley floor of seemingly lifeless orange desert

The skiing is remote and uncompromising above the tree-line.

and sage brush wound down to the plateau which continued as far as the horizon. In the other, a huge mountain soared from the plateau into the heavens.

The wind was getting stronger, blowing in quite violent gusts, whipping the snow from the mountain and exposing the naked Andes rock. Where it had reached the snow and made it crusty, it was difficult to turn. Like any major mountain range, the Andes can change its mood in a matter of moments. The wind was now gusting ferociously, the sun was beginning to sink towards the horizon and there were jagged rocks sticking through the snow. It was time to return to base.

Back at the most comfortable of Las Lenas's hotels, the Piscis – complete with casino, swimming pool, jacuzzi, sauna, massage parlour, restaurants, bars, shops and even a theatre – it was time to look around. You are given a plastic credit card which you can use to purchase anything in the resort. Your account is settled when you leave.

Las Lenas has one bizarre claim to fame: it is only sixteen kilometres (ten miles) from the area where an airliner crashed in the seventies and its passengers resorted to cannibalism in order to stay alive. Parts of the wrecked fuselage are still visible during the summer. One method of reaching Las Lenas from Buenos Aires 1180 kilometres (730 miles) away is to take the Ski Lenas aeroplane. Your ticket covers the return flight, half-board accommodation and even your lift pass. It takes two hours to get to Marlague airport, from where you complete your journey by bus.

Marlague, set in the arid desert, is about eighty kilometres (fifty miles) from Las Lenas. On the homeward leg, flying via Rio de Janeiro appeals to many travellers. It is then possible to visit the spectacular Iguazu Falls, which drop over 275 precipices during a 2.75-kilometre arc. No matter how good the skiing, it would after all be rather a waste to travel such a distance without seeing at

least something of the other fascinating and exotic attractions of South America.

North America is an increasingly popular destination for European skiers, and resorts in South America too are beginning to catch their imagination. One day, perhaps, it may become almost as common to take a skiing holiday in Las Lenas as La Plagne.

But why wait until then?

The volatile Andes – not to be taken lightly.

Below
Pyramids in the Argentinian snow. It could almost be part of a purpose-built French resort.

HAPPO ONE

Japan has hundreds of ski resorts, and without skiing them all – which would obviously take several winters – it is not easy to select the best, especially when you discover that every Japanese skier you speak to seems to have different views on the subject.

I have chosen Happo One, on the slopes of Karamatsu (2696 metres; 8,845 feet) in the Hakuba Valley because the skiing is good and it is also one of the largest skiing areas in Japan, with more than thirty million 'skier days' (a measurement based on the number of lift passes issued during the season, which in Happo One's case is from mid December until mid May). Resorts like Vail, Colorado – one

of America's biggest ski areas – have something in excess of three million skier days, although this has a lot more to do with Japan's population than the relative size of the ski areas.

Skiing was introduced to Japan in 1910 by the Austrians, and an incredible number of Japanese – twelve million – now ski.

Japan's mountain terrain is very much moulded by its volcanic origins. The rock structure is relatively young, with sharp, newly eroded edges and shallow bowl summits. The tree-line extends to just above 1524 metres (5,000 feet), which covers most of the skiable terrain – so most of the runs are cut trails through the forests and reminiscent of the ski area on America's east coast.

With its strongly maritime climate, and the same latitude as the area between Morocco and the south of France, Japan's snow conditions tend to be quite changeable. It is interesting to note that Japan has also been experiencing the same parsimonious precipitation at the start of the recent skiing seasons in Europe. Japan's weather pattern is even further complicated by the influence of mainland China – but Japanese resorts can experience the most wonderful powder conditions.

Strange to relate the Japanese tend to avoid powder skiing, which is, in my view rather like a wine buff avoiding champagne. But it does mean that European skiers can avoid the teeming hordes of local skiers and sometimes help themselves to acres of unbelievably light and fluffy powder that would be skied out in a day in European resorts.

Another way to avoid the crowds is to ski during your lunch hour. At midday almost everyone stops what they are doing and forms huge queues for curried rice at the nearest mountain restaurant.

In fairness, one has to put the record straight about the commonly held belief that Japanese ski slopes are crowded with skiers all tuned in to their Sony Walkmen. It is true that at weekends this is often the case, especially in resorts close to the big cities, where it can become pandemonium by midday. In Nozawa Onsen, for example, the buses start rumbling at 4.30 am on Saturdays, having been on the road all night. Some weekend skiers are so keen that they are prepared to drive for eight to twelve hours each way. They can – if really desperate – even ski all night too to make it worth their while at resorts like Naeba (number five in my list of Japan's top ten resorts.) But during the week, it is quite possible to find relatively uncrowded slopes.

It was Hannes Schneider, the father of the Austrian school of skiing, who helped shape the Japanese dedication to skiing and their thorough approach to technique, although as a people they already possessed a natural flair for the meticulous and the ritualistic.

Resorts such as Happo One, Siga Heights, Kutsatau, Nozawa Onsen, Naeba and Zao are located along the principal mountain chain on the island of Honshu and are thus destination resorts for skiers from the capital, Tokyo. The northern island of Hokaido – which was host to the Winter Olympics of 1972 at Sapporo – has some of Japan's biggest ski areas.

The journey to Hakuba takes a little under five hours by train from Tokyo. You leave on the express train from Shinjuku station and change at Matsumoto. Here you board a train for Hakuba. On the way it is possible to visit one of the local tourist attractions – macaque monkeys who bathe in the hot volcanic spring waters to stay warm in winter. The monkeys – among the most northerly dwelling of their species – have their homes surrounded by deep snow in winter, but they survive by swimming and living in their natural hot tub.

Skiers find Japan's hot sulphur baths a therapeutic experience too. In the open-air variety – rotenboro – you can drink sake while gazing at the moon and stars. But unlike the monkeys, skiers tend not to want to stay the entire night. Mind you, almost equally unusual sleeping arrangements can be found in some Japanese accommodation: you may find tatami (rush) matting rolled out on the floor accompanied by cushions in the centre of the room which can sleep up to five people in a sort of Busby Berkeley arrangement.

Hukaba is a large area by any standards, with six gelande (a word they borrowed from their Austrian skiing mentors which means ski grounds). There is a cable car and twenty-four lifts. The skiing terrain is fascinatingly different. There are little cliffs with deep, soft landings, hidden groves of gnarled trees, and untracked slopes packed with fresh powder.

The most challenging run is probably the Riesen slalom. Experienced skiers can make a 2000-metre (6,560 feet) descent in testing conditions by turning left under the cable car (not advisable from its famous Chamonix equivalent, the Aiguille du Midi, where turning left brings an immediate and invariably fatal fall of 3000 metres; 9,840 feet).

It is not always easy to unravel the translations of some Japanese ski runs. I was amused to learn from Simon Halewood, of the Japanese Tourist Office in London, that 'for some reason the further up into the mountains you go, the more mysterious and obscure the names become.' However, other good runs include Skyline, International Gelande and Usuki-Daira which has some of the deepest snow.

Diana Mathias, a British ski instructor who has skied in several Japanese resorts says: 'The people are very traditional, polite and most hospitable, and friendly. The skiing is beautiful and the mountains are dramatic.'

This is echoed by two other instructors, Doug Godlington and Hazel Bain, who found the friendliness of the Japanese 'overwhelming.' And my colleague Philip Milner-Barry says:

The Japanese never forget their manners. Someone does an unexpected turn in front of you, you swerve, tripping up the person behind you and causing him to take to the air, perform a triple somersault, and end on his back with his head downhill and his skis gone to heaven-knows-where. So long as consciousness remains, he will find the strength to raise his head, look you squarely in the eye, and apologise.

If only that happened in Europe!

Happo One, in the Hakuba Valley, is one of the largest skiing areas in Japan.

LAST RESORT

If I were to attempt to identify the world's top fifty ski resorts in the year 2000, it might be quite a different collection of places from the one I have put together for this book. Although the giants such as Val d'Isère, Vail and Verbier will no doubt go from strength to strength, there are a number of new ski areas being developed which could assume world importance.

In Gulmarg, for example, India's best-known resort in the Himalayas above Srinagar, the construction of a cable car up to the summit of the Affervat would transform the skiing.

At the time of writing, the resort is neither one thing nor the other. There are three or four lifts suitable for beginners or very modest intermediates. And at the other extreme there is huge potential stored in the mountains for helicopter skiing which the French ski extreme specialist Sylvain Saudan has been investigating. What the resort needs desperately to turn it into a 'serious' ski resort is the essential 'middle-ground' of some good intermediate skiing which the planned cable car would bring. Until that happens it is only going to attract either mice or machos.

Coronet Peak in New Zealand is building up a great reputation, especially for its helicopter skiing. There are those who believe it already deserves a place in the world's best. Mount Hutt is another ski area in New Zealand which is starting to command attention.

And in Australia, resorts such as Thredbo and Perisher Valley are popular with the locals, and although it is difficult to imagine that they will ever become major ski resorts, they have their own special beauty and fascination.

Australia's mountains are low by world standards. Mount Kosciusko, for example – the highest in the Snowy Mountains – only reaches 2228 metres (7,310 feet), a mere quarter of the height of Everest. Victoria's tallest mountains – Mount Bogong, Mount Feathertop and Mount Hotham – are all below 2000 metres (6,562 feet). But small can still be beautiful. The rugged lower slopes of the Australian Alps are covered with thick forests of tall eucalyptus. In winter as much as 7000 square kilometres (4,350 square miles) may be covered with a thick blanket of snow, forming the most extensive snowfields in Australia. The smooth, silhouetted curves of the white-capped mountains look particularly attractive when they are illuminated by a full moon or a spectacular sunset. But the weather is very unpredictable. Snowfall varies enormously from year to year. Sometimes there is little snow even in the winter months. During other years blizzards have been experienced in the summer.

Many dedicated skiers – including me – regard helicopter skiing in the Canadian Rockies as the best in the world. You cannot really call the classic ski areas like the Bugaboos, Cariboos and Monashees ski resorts, even though each has a hundred classic off-piste descents available to helicopter skiers staying at remote mountain lodges. If you could call them resorts they would all occupy pride of place in this book.

And what of Russia and China? My trip to Bakuriani in Georgia gave me little real insight into Russian skiing except that the equipment was antiquated and the skiing limited. But the potential is undoubtedly there. I cannot pretend to know anything about skiing in China, but there must be endless potential.

Nor have I skied in the Lebanon, where a beautiful ski area is, as far as I know, difficult and risky to reach for the average skier because of the mindless destruction and carnage that has been tearing Beirut apart. In February 1989, the fighting spread to the slopes when fourteen Christian and Lebanese troops were injured in a brawl at Faraya.

Having scratched the surface of the skiing in India and Russia as well as skiing much more intensively in Europe and North America, I would love to ski in more of these exotic, far-away places – such as Iran where even on the slopes the sexes are segregated and apres ski is non-alcoholic by order – not because they might turn out to be among the world's best (almost certainly they will not) but because I love the different flavours of

Heli-skiing – the only real way up to the virgin powder.

the various skiing environments and national characteristics.

Where else but in India would you get a sherpa to carry your skis up the mountain, later to descend by toboggan with your guide while you make the best of coming down on skis with no edges and boots with broken clips, held together with fuse wire?

And where else but in Scotland would the ski-lift attendant stand on a box because of lack of snow and, in driving sleet, reach for your T-bar with an umbrella?

Where else but in the American Rockies would people ski in cowboy hats and form orderly lift lines without pushing and shoving?

And where else but in Japan would a skier you had just mown down take great pains to climb back on to his feet and apologize to *you*?

Skiing is a wonderful way of encountering the planet, some of its most stunning scenery, and some of its most interesting people. As I prepare to explore the snows of Australia, Japan and South America, what intrigues me about other solar systems is not whether life exists there, but what the skiing is like.

Acknowledgements

With special thanks to **Joe Kirwin**

Hazel Bain
Sandy Barker (Luhta)
Harry Baxter and Kari Gemmel (Jackson Hole Ski Corporation)
Anita Benson
Franz Blum (Swiss National Tourist Office)
Mark Chitty (Mark Warner)
Minty Clinch
Delta Airlines
Doug Godlington
Charles Hallifax
Peter Hardy and Felice Eyston (Skishoot)
Mark Heller
Tom Hermens (Sports International)
Elisabeth Hussey (Ski Survey)
Siegbert Kuchling (Austrian Airlines)

Richard King
Eddie Laxton
Gina Lamb (Fleet PR)
Nigel Lloyd
Colin Murison-Small (Small World)
Robin Neillands
Sean O'Beirne (Collineige)
Sue Ockwell
Stephen Pooley
The Swiss Travel Service
Chris Tizzard
Gloria Ward (Thomson Holidays)
Anita Webber (Ski Inghams)
Bernie Weichsel (Ski the USA)
Veronica Wilson
and
Alyson Gregory, my editor

Picture Credits

NORTH AMERICA
Alta: Alta Ski Area; Lee Cohen
Aspen: Aspen Ski Company; Tom Martin; Norm Clasen
Breckenridge: Breckenridge Ski Area; Carl Scofield
Heavenly Valley: Heavenly Valley Ski Area; Joe Kirwin
Jackson Hole: Jackson Hole Ski Resort; Bob Woodall; James W Kay
Killington: Killington Ski Resort
Mammoth: Mammoth/June Ski Resort; Peatross
Park City: Park City Ski Corporation
Snowbird: Snowbird Ski Resort; Chris Noble; Ed Blankman
Snowmass: Aspen Ski Company; Pat Collins
Squaw Valley: Squaw Valley Ski Corporation; Hank de Vré
Stowe: Stowe Ski Area
Sun Valley: Sun Valley Company; Joe Kirwin

Taos: Taos Ski Valley; Ken Gallard
Telluride: Telluride Ski Resort; Linde Waidhofer
Vail: Vail Associates; David Lokey
Banff/Lake Louise: Lake Louise Ski Area; Joe Kirwin
Whistler/Blackcomb: Whistler Resort Association

EUROPE
Chamonix: Ian Barr
Austrian Tourist Office
French Government Tourist Office
Italian State Tourist Office
Swiss National Tourist Office

GENERAL
Skier Magazine
Skishoot
VFB Holidays